T0266542

REVISED EDITION

ALASKA'S
WILD PLANTS

A Guide to Alaska's Edible and Healthful Harvest

JANICE J. SCHOFIELD

ALASKA
NORTHWEST
BOOKS®

Dedicated to the wild plants,
who are our greatest teachers,
and to all who love and cherish them.

A portion of the proceeds from the sale of this book benefits
Kachemak Heritage Land Trust, a non-profit corporation dedicated
to preservation of critical habitat in the Kachemak region.
For additional information on KHLT, write 315 Klondike Avenue,
Homer, AK 99603, or go to www.kachemaklandtrust.org.

Text and photographs © 2020 by Janice J. Schofield

Edited by Susan Sommer
Indexed by Sam Arnold-Boyd

Library of Congress Cataloging-in-Publication Data

Names: Eaton, Janice Schofield, 1951- author.
Title: Alaska's wild plants : a guide to Alaska's edible and healthful harvest / Janice J. Schofield.
Description: Revised edition. | [Berkeley, Calif.] : Alaska Northwest Books, an imprint of West
    Margin Press, [2020] | Includes bibliographical references and index. | Summary: "An
    introductory field guide to the most common edible plants in Alaska, including photographs
    and information on each plant's botanical name, harvesting direction, food and medicinal
    use, and more"—Provided by publisher.
Identifiers: LCCN 2019049578 (print) | LCCN 2019049579 (ebook) | ISBN 9781513262789
    (paperback) | ISBN 9781513262796 (hardback) | ISBN 9781513262802 (ebook)
Subjects: LCSH: Wild plants, Edible—Alaska—Identification. | Wild plants, Edible—Therapeutic
    use—Alaska. | Cooking (Wild foods)—Alaska.
Classification: LCC QK98.5.U6 E28 2020 (print) | LCC QK98.5.U6 (ebook) |
    DDC 581.6/3209798—dc23
LC record available at https://lccn.loc.gov/2019049578
LC ebook record available at https://lccn.loc.gov/2019049579

Printed in the United States of America
3 4 5 6 7 8 9 10

Proudly distributed by Ingram Publisher Services

Alaska Northwest Books®
An imprint of Turner Publishing Company
4507 Charlotte Avenue, Suite 100
Nashville, TN 37209
(615) 255-2665
www.turnerbookstore.com

WESTMARGIN PRESS
Publishing Director: Jennifer Newens
Marketing Manager: Angela Zbornik
Editor: Olivia Ngai
Design & Production: Rachel Lopez Metzger

CONTENTS

TUNDRA

MEADOWS

MARSHES, PONDS, CREEKS & WETLANDS

POISONOUS PLANTS

INTRODUCTION

Over two and a half decades have passed since the original publication of *Alaska's Wild Plants*. During that time, interest in wild plants has soared. More enthusiasts than ever flock to plant classes, buy plant books, and head to the wild. The motivation for many is similar to what first stirred me to forage: supplementary and emergency food, and deeper connection to plants and the natural world.

Alaska is an extreme place to live with its short, intense growing season. In the endless summer light, plants gallop from sprout to seed. Though more and more tunnel houses have been erected in Alaskan towns and villages for extending the gardening season, the hardy wild remains a source of nutrient dense plants, combined with the fun of gathering.

Alaska is also where outdoor adventurers abound and there is higher risk of getting lost, stranded, or injured out in the wild. Knowing how to use the wild green helpers for first aid can be lifesaving. This revised updated edition expands knowledge of using herbs for health purposes. See page 182 for directions on preparing herbal poultices, ointments, infusions, decoctions, and tinctures.

Foraging requires developing observational skills like learning to recognize plants in varying stages of growth. Gatherers must differentiate between the herbal helpers and the inedible plants. This book is intended as one guide in your journey.

A book of this size, ideal for the backpack and replete with details of how to incorporate these plants into your life, cannot also be an exhaustive guide to identification. It's intended as an adjunct to heftier tomes like *Discovering Wild Plants* (with detailed line drawings by R.W. Tyler and photos of the plants throughout the growing season), Beverly Gray's *The Boreal Herbal*, Verna Pratt's many photographic guides, and academic plant keys. Countless online reference materials are also available. If you have any doubt of a plant's identity, cross-check with other sources. See page 190 for my recommended reading.

How This Book is Organized

Plants, like people, live in communities. Plants that flourish together share affinity for certain soils, lighting conditions, moisture, salinity, or altitude. For this reason, this book is organized by habitat. Once you find one of the plants in a section, you are likely to meet many of the companions listed. Beach plants, for example, will be not be found anywhere except near ocean shores.

However, some plants, like blueberry, are highly adaptable. Blueberries range from bog to forest to alpine. Hence, a new category in this edition has been added: Free-Range Plants. This section is an excellent starting point for readers, as it also develops awareness of the floral patterns of plant families like mustard. Learn to recognize the characteristic structure of a mustard flower, and a vast "friendly family" of plants is at your service.

Within each section, plants are grouped by similar type. In Sea & Sandy Shores, the seaweeds sequentially follow each other, then the shore plants. Within Forests & Open Woods, all the trees are sequential, followed by the understory plants.

The habitat sections are explained in detail at the beginning of each new segment of the book. Each section is also coded with a color for easy reference.

Before You Begin

1 Review the Caution sections carefully. Some plants, such as cow parsnip, can cause dermatitis; others, like red elder, have both edible and toxic portions.

2 When eating any new food for the first time, consume a small amount only. Be sensitive to the effect on your body; discontinue use immediately and seek medical attention if you experience adverse reactions or allergies.

3 Just because something is "good for you" in moderation and seasonally available, it doesn't mean consuming gallons a day of that thing will be better. Be sensible.

4 If you are pregnant or on pharmaceuticals, and have questions regarding whether a particular herb is suitable for you, check with your health professional. Some online sources show cautions for virtually anything and everything and are not always accurate.

5 Start slowly and build confidence plant by plant. Included in this book are numerous recipe ideas to stimulate your creativity.

After the Harvest

1 Rinse your edibles in cool water to remove dust. If using roots, scrub them well with a brush.

2 For year-round use, bundle herbs and hang upside down in a warm, shady, well-ventilated space. (An exception are sea vegetables, which often mold unless quickly sun-dried.)

3 Herbs, including small quantities of sea vegetables, may also be dried in an oven on the lowest setting, or in an electric or solar-powered dehydrator.

4 When the herbs are fully dried, store them in a dark place in airtight containers. Label and date.

5 Storage life is generally 6 months to 1 year for green, leafy herbs, and 1 to 3 years for roots. Supplement these guidelines by comparing the herb's color, taste, odor, and effectiveness to when it was first dried.

Basic Foraging Principles

1 Be 100% positive of identification. If in doubt, don't.

2 Harvest only what you can use and process.

3 Gather plants in clean areas, away from busy roadsides and toxic sprays.

4 Avoid wrestling with the plant. If the plant part won't release without a struggle, let it be. It's probably not "ripe" (or willing). Move on to another plant.

5 Gather only where it's legal. Off limits to foragers are Alaskan state, national, and municipal parks. Harvesting is allowed on state land not designated as parkland, provided that you collect 50 feet back from the highway. In national forests, stay 200 feet back from established trails, roads, and campgrounds. Ask permission to harvest on private land. Be aware that some regions have local laws in place for harvesting; for example, seaweed harvest has closure areas in Cook Inlet. (See Sea & Sandy Shores on page 31 for details.)

6 Know the toxic lookalikes. Study the Poisonous Plants section thoroughly. A nibble of poison hemlock could have dire consequences.

7 Monitor the impact of your foraging. Whenever possible, return year after year to your favorite gathering area. When digging roots, begin by collecting only 1 or 2 out of 10 roots from productive patches. You may discover that some roots, like dandelion, may seemingly defy depletion. Expand your harvesting quotas as appropriate for each species.

In a conference lecture many moons ago, herbalist Susun S. Weed said that plants that grow in greatest abundance around us are shouting for our attention and welcoming our use. Rather than spray these "weeds" with herbicides or evict them to the dump, we can enthusiastically use them. The nettles, chickweeds, lamb's quarters, and dandelions are better than a vitamin tablet, and freely available.

Such nutrient-dense plants fall in the category of "tonic" herbs and can be consumed daily as food and teas. They are the superfoods that strengthen and tone our body systems. You can buy expensive foreign goji berries or harvest Alaska's wild berries for free. Purchase spirulina, or harvest nettles and process their powder for green smoothies.

These tonic plants typify the wisdom in the quote (often attributed to Hippocrates): "Let food be thy medicine, and let medicine be thy food."

The concept of "tonic, specific, and heroic herbs" was introduced to me by Robyn Klein of Bozeman Montana Sweetgrass School of Herbalism.

It offers a framework for herbal safety.

Some plants included in this book, like coltsfoot (*Petasites* species) and wormwood (*Artemisia tilesii*) are classified as "specifics." These herbs require thoughtful use. This category includes plants used to address a specific health condition, and they are ingested for a specific period of time (generally several days to a week). Wormwood is specific for colds or flu. Coltsfoot is specific for bronchitis and respiratory congestion.

The third class, "heroic" herbs, is included in the Poisonous Plants section on page 175. Though some of these plants have use in pharmacy and clinical herbalism, detailing such advanced use is beyond the scope of this book. Incorrect dosing could potentially result in death.

Learning More About a Plant & Notes on Botanical Names

If you want to look up more information on a plant, it is essential to do so by **botanical name**. This book provides for each plant the name of the genus and species, and family, listed in that order. Algae also list their division. Common names for plants vary widely, even within Alaska. Wild celery, for example, is used regionally for *Heracleum lanatum* (cow parsnip), *Ligusticum scoticum* (beach lovage), and *Angelica* species (Angelica).

Genus and species names are often derived from the Latin or Greek, and some names, translated, describe the plant or its properties. *Urtica* (stinging nettle), for example, is from the Latin *uro*, "to burn." *Streptopus amplexifolius* (twisted stalk) literally means "the twisted stalk with the clasping leaf."

If you're intimidated about proper pronunciation of botanical names, relax. "As anyone who has worked with a lot of professional botanists knows," writes seedsman J.L. Hudson, "there is no agreement among them as to the correct pronunciation of names, and everyone pronounces them however they like." Just say them with confidence.

Even if all you can pinpoint is the former botanical name, this book, Wikipedia, Thomas J. Elpel's *Botany in a Day*, or other resources will still guide you to your desired plant.

You may notice that some plants in this book have changed genus completely (fireweed is now *Chamerion* instead of *Epilobium*). Families have flipflopped around and many now have "tribes" and "sub-tribes." This is because botanists are now using DNA analysis to determine relationships of one plant to another, rather than just the patterns of flower arrangement.

But don't fret about what the botanists are doing. Whether or not you can "key" a plant botanically, or recognize all the plants by family, you can still become skilled at safely identifying plants.

My grandmother, and indigenous plant people throughout Alaska, did not have access to academic plant keys. Yet they were phenomenal herbalists. They used their senses, and their common sense.

Using Herbs in Our Everyday Life is Our Birthright

Medical herbalist Richard Whelan points out that "the reason that herbs can never be patented and owned by any individual or corporation is because they are, and always will be, the People's medicine." And Montana herbalist Robyn Klein reminds us that our right to use herbs or other botanicals is protected by the Dietary Supplement Health and Education Act of 1994 passed by Congress.

Learning to use herbs for ourselves, our families, our animals, and our communities is a life skill worthy of developing.

Perhaps you're like me, raised in the "time of the great forgetting" of herbal knowledge. Growing up in New England in the 1950s, my parents treated our cuts and scrapes with mercurochrome or a pharmacy antiseptic. Upset stomachs earned a dose of hot-pink Pepto-Bismol®. More serious illnesses triggered doctor's visits and penicillin. It wasn't until decades later that I learned that my father's mother (who I never got to meet) had been an herbalist. For grandmother Eugenie, herbs were her allies. The kids' colds and flu were soothed with yarrow, and wounds with plantain poultices.

Today I follow in her footsteps, using the exact same herbal allies for tending my family and livestock, along with a much-broadened repertoire of local wild plants for enhanced well-being. Looking back, after 4 decades of incorporating "wild things" into my life, I can attest to the benefits of these nutrient-dense foods. Though eating weeds and wild plants can't guarantee ongoing health, they certainly can help stack odds in your favor. My parents both had adult onset diabetes when they were 2 decades younger than I am now. I'm thankfully still free of pharmaceuticals.

The act of foraging in nature makes use of the best doctors in the world. As described in the nursery rhyme:

"The best six doctors anywhere and no one can deny it
Are sunshine, water, rest, and air, exercise and diet."

Foraging the wild weaves together all these elements. So be sensible, but be unafraid. Put your toe in the earth and start foraging. May you experience deep health and happiness, as you enjoy the pursuit of herbs.

Free-Range Plants

The plants I dub the "free rangers" are extremely adaptable and difficult to pin down to any one habit. With mustards, for example, I address the entire forager-friendly family in one entry. Some mustards tend to favor beaches, others open rocky places, and some prefer your garden soil. Listing them under one habitat is far too limiting. And plants like coltsfoot mystified me, as our first encounter was in open forest, by a creek. Then I discovered it thriving in a sunny meadow. And later, in the mountains on rocky scree slopes. In Kotzebue, coltsfoot is prolific on the tundra. So coltsfoot, shown here below, is now another of the free-range plants.

WILD MUSTARD
Mustard family (Brassicaceae, formerly Cruciferae family)

BRASSICA

MUSTARD FLOWER (ROCKCRESS)

SPOONWORT

SHEPHERD'S PURSE

Alaska's mustards are highly variable in genera, habitat, leaf shape, and in the shape of their seedpods. The good news is that the entire family is highly "friendly" to foragers. Moreover, all mustard flowers have an easily recognizable floral pattern: 4 petals, with 6 yellow thread-like male stamens—of which 4 are tall and 2 are short. As a memory boost, remember: "4 fine fellows with 2 tiny tims." The female portion is the pistil. Mustard pistils mature into the seedpods of remarkable variety. To see mustard's floral characteristics well, use a pocket loupe (magnifier). Most wild mustards have small flowers, but pods and flowers are often visible at the same time. After a short while, you will just begin to spot mustards at a glance wherever you go, even in your own backyard. All of Alaska's mustards are safe to nibble, though not every single species appeals to the palate, the highly bitter "wormseed" (*Erysimum*) being my personal "yuck" on edibility. But as long as you can positively discern "mustard" and your plant passes your palatability test, you're good to go.

14

Common to cultivated and disturbed soils are mustards including the ubiquitous yellow-flowered Brassicas (commonly called wild mustard or rapeseed), and the tasty rockcress, aka wild cress (*Arabis* species).

Spoonwort, aka scurvygrass (*Cochlearia officinalis*). This is a round- to spoon-leafed beach mustard whose leaves add zest and vitamin C to coastal camping meals.

Shepherd's purse (*Capsella bursa-pastoris*) is exceptionally easy to recognize with its distinctive heart-shaped seedpods. Petals are white. The peppery-tasting stem leaves are arrow shaped and alternate along the stem. The lower leaves, like those of dandelions, are deeply lobed and arranged in a basal rosette, i.e. they grow in a circular pattern at the base of the stem.

Other commonly eaten Alaskan mustards include:

- Bittercress, aka spring cress (*Cardamine* species) has white- to rose-colored flowers and long narrow seedpods (siliques).

- Sea rocket, aka beach rocket (*Cakile edentula*). A pink-petaled beach species with leaves with wavy or saw-toothed edges.

Refer to *Discovering Wild Plants* for detailed illustrations and line drawings of these and other Alaskan mustard species.

RANGE: Mustards range throughout all regions of Alaska and in diverse habitats.

HARVESTING DIRECTIONS: Leaves are prime before flowering; flavor becomes stronger and more peppery with age. Selectively pick flowers and seedpods throughout the summer, leaving some remaining on the plant to propagate.

FOOD USE: Leaves add zest to salads, stir-fries, and soups. Seeds and roots are traditional spices. Blend mustard with cream cheese as a dip; dairy-free foragers can blend chopped mustard (leaves, young pods, seeds) with ground, soaked cashews, nutritional yeast, lemon, and salt.

HEALTH USE: Mustards in general are good sources of vitamins A and C, and the minerals calcium, potassium, and manganese. Shepherd's purse, in particular, is an excellent source of blood-clotting vitamin K, making it of use in the field as a poultice for cuts. Shepherd's purse tea has traditionally been drunk to soothe stomach ulcers and can be applied with a cotton swab to hemorrhoids.

OTHER: Tulane University, in the 1970s, conducted experiments documenting that shepherd's purse seeds, placed in water, release a gummy exudate that entraps and destroys mosquito larvae.

BLUEBERRY & HUCKLEBERRY
Vaccinium species
Heath family (Ericaceae), Blueberry subfamily (Vaccinioideae)

FLOWER STAGE

FRUIT STAGE

Alaska's blueberries, aka bilberries, are truly free-rangers, growing in acid soils in woods, wet meadows, heaths, bogs, and in the mountains to over 3,000 feet. "Mother's Day flowers" is a common name for the bell-like pinkish to whitish blooms that generally flower in early May. These shrubby plants range from low tufted varieties to species more than 3 feet high. *Vaccinium* fruits are blue to bluish-black, with a couple exceptions: *Vaccinium parvifolium*, red huckleberry found only in south coastal to Southeast Alaska, and the dwarf red-fruited lingonberry, aka lowbush cranberry, *Vaccinium vitis-idaea* (see page 114).

DERIVATION OF NAME: *Vaccinium* is the classical name for blueberry and cranberry.

OTHER NAMES: huckleberry, great bilberry, whortleberry, dyeberry, wineberry, Mother's Day flowers.

RANGE: Throughout Alaska except the extreme north Arctic.

HARVESTING DIRECTIONS: The early blooming flowers are edible and sweet, but most gatherers prefer waiting for the delectable fruits!

FOOD USE: Nibble *Vaccinium* blooms to savor their refreshing, light, blueberry tang. Toss a few blossoms on a salad or dip as a garnish. Limit your flower intake to ensure abundant fruits. Snack on the berries in the field while gathering. Bake in pies. Mix into a morning smoothie. Add to pancakes, muffins. biscuits, nut breads, salads. Make jam or juice. How about a blueberry vinaigrette, marinade, or liquor?

HEALTH USE: A study published in the *International Journal of Circumpolar Health* noted antioxidant values of *Vacciniums* and other berries. Values were compared using an ORAC scale (Oxygen Radical Absorption Capacity). The higher the ORAC value, the more antioxidants to protect the body against cellular damage that can lead to cancer, heart disease, and Alzheimer's. Interestingly, while cultivated blueberries rank 30 on the ORAC scale and Lower 48 wild blueberries rank 61, Alaskan wild blueberries test a stunning 85. Blueberries have hypoglycemic and antidiabetic activity and are a valuable aid to those experiencing excess weight. Statistically, 32% of Americans classify as obese, and indigenous populations are particularly at risk. Trials published in the *Journal of Agricultural and Food Chemistry* document blueberry's abundant anthrocyanins, which "actively regulate genetic markers associated with obesity. Rats on high fat diets failed to get obese in the presence of the compounds so richly available in blueberries." Blueberries also contain proanthocyanins, compounds having antiadhesion and antiproliferation properties, effective in easing urinary tract infections. For urinary tract infections while in the bush, young leaves (with a tart aftertaste) are often blended with blueberries and drunk 2 to 3 cups a day for up to a week.

OTHER: Blueberries are a valued subsistence food for Native communities and bush residents, both culturally and nutritionally. Blending blueberries with sugar and seal oil is a traditional Iñupiaq dessert. And blueberry pickled fish is another favorite. "Any meat or fat stored in blueberries" writes Anore Jones, "will get pickled, flavored, and brilliantly colored in a few days to a week."

LOOKALIKES: Some foragers have been fooled by finding bell-like blooms on shrubby false azalea (*Menzisia ferrugina*), only to return at berry time to find no berries! Aptly called "fool's blueberry," this plant is a good teacher in observation as its family pattern is quite different from the *Vacciniums*.

COLTSFOOT
Petasites species
Aster family (Asteraceae), Groundsel tribe (Senecioneae)

FREE-RANGE PLANTS

Coltsfoot is wide ranging and widely loved in Native villages throughout Alaska. Habitats vary from moist places in woods to Arctic tundra to rocky mountain passes. Its nickname "son before father" refers to coltsfoot's unusual habit of flowering before the leaves develop. The fragrant cluster of blossoms sits atop a rather thick and hairy stem. Leaves vary from triangular to lobed and bear a thick felt-like covering on their undersides. All species are equally useable.

DERIVATION OF NAME: *Petasites* translates as "broad-brimmed hat" and refers, rather imaginatively, to the shape of the leaves.

OTHER NAMES: sweet coltsfoot, *qaltaruat* and *pellukutar* (Yup'ik), *kipmimanggaun* (Iñupiaq, Kotzebue), *k'ijeghi ch'da* (Dena'ina/Tanaina, "owl's blanket"), penicillin plant (Iliamna area), son before father.

RANGE: Throughout Alaska. *Petasites frigidus* and *P. hyperboreus* can be found from the far north to the end of the Alaska Peninsula and to the Canadian Border. *P. palmatus* and *P. sagittatus* are mainly found in the eastern half of the state.

HARVESTING DIRECTIONS: Pick coltsfoot flowers in very early spring, before they start to turn brown. Leaves are safest for harvesting later in summer (when pyrrolizidine alkaloids are lowest; see Caution below). Rootstalks are dug spring or fall.

FOOD USE: Coltsfoot flowers are one of the earliest spring wild foods. During a June plant class in Kotzebue years ago, coltsfoot flowers emerging from the exceptionally late snowmelt starred in our soups, stir-fries, spring rolls, and tempura. Young leaves, in small quantities, were also added. In *Flora of Alaska*, Eric Hultén notes that roots were roasted and eaten by the Siberian Eskimos.

HEALTH USE: Coltsfoot has a plethora of names culturally, but a commonality of use. It is a "specific" herb for acute respiratory congestion and cramps. *Petasites* species contain the antispasmodic petasin. Leaf syrup provided dramatic relief when I experienced an acute bronchitis at my wilderness cabin. Indigenous people chew the root (and swallow the juice) for easing sore throat. Root decoctions and tinctures are used to ease asthma attacks. In addition, herbalists favor coltsfoot teas for stress-aggravated stomach cramps. Alaskan west coast Yup'ik also use leaf tea for stomach pain and diarrhea. Use of coltsfoot for relief of menstrual cramps is reported by Kodiak Alutiiq as well.

OTHER: A standardized root extract Petadolex demonstrates effectiveness in migraine prevention. The *International Journal of Clinical Pharmacology and Therapeutics* published a clinical trial in which, "the frequency of migraine attacks decreased by a maximum of 60% compared to the baseline." (Note: this pharmaceutic formulation removes the P.A. alkaloids discussed in the following caution, thus deemed safe for long-term use.)

CAUTION: Coltsfoot has been safely used for centuries by diverse people taking it short term for easing acute respiratory distress and cramps. Coltsfoot contains pyrrolizidine alkaloids (P.A.), which, in excess, can damage the liver. Herbalist Kathi Keville reports that in Germany, the recommended maximum dose of coltsfoot is 1 teaspoon dry herb daily for a maximum of 1 month. If pregnant, check with your physician before ingesting.

DANDELION
Taraxacum species
Aster family (Asteraceae), Chicory subfamily (Cichorioideae)

Alaska has 11 dandelion species that free range from backyards to tundra to alpine. Species include the "common dandelion" of Eurasian origin *Taxaracum officinale* (used globally as food and medicine), the rare Alaska-only nodding dandelion (*T. carneocoloratum*) of scree slopes, and Alaska dandelion (*T. alaskanum*) of alpine and tundra, etc. All dandelions are forager friendly, though nodding dandelion should be spared because of its rarity. Dandelions bear yellow composite blossoms with only 1 blossom per stem (be certain to differentiate from false dandelions, which have stems that branch). Break a dandelion stem and it yields a milky sap. The smooth leaves have jagged edges, hence their French name *dent-de-lion*, or lion-tooth; tooth depth varies with species. Though taproots are normally a few inches deep, a Palmer student grew roots 2 feet long in her raised bed. *Taraxacum* roots have been recorded to penetrate the earth to a depth of 20 feet.

DERIVATION OF NAME: *Taraxacum* means "remedy for disorder."

OTHER NAMES: blowball, dent-de-lion, pissenlit.

RANGE: Diverse habitats throughout Alaska.

HARVESTING DIRECTIONS: Leaves are most mild flavored early spring before flowering, and in autumn when new growth occurs. Plants in the shade tend to be milder tasting. Pick buds as available, and flowers in full bloom. However, if you intend to dry the flowers, harvest when just beginning to open; they will continue to "mature" while drying. If you dry fully open flowers, they will turn to seed. Dig roots early spring and late fall; brush firmly to remove dirt, and rinse well.

FOOD USE: Add mild dandelion leaves to salads, spring rolls, stir-fries, soups, and scrambled eggs. Rub with olive oil and sprinkles of salt and seasonings and dry as a snack chip. Blend dandelion with lamb's quarter, chickweed, sorrel, and tomato juice as a refreshing elixir. Marinate summer leaves as salad or try the Tlingit way of cooking leaves in a change of salted water to remove any bitterness. Pickle buds like capers. Dandelion flower petals (pinch off and discard the green sepals) are a delightful salad garnish: mix with salmon, onion, rice, and your favorite seasonings and cook as a burger. I love greeting the morning with "dandelion expresso." Roast dry chopped dandelion root in a cast iron skillet until desired degree of roast is achieved. Roots become highly aromatic (be careful not to burn). Then grind and use in an espresso maker or simmer 1 tablespoon of the roasted root per cup (starting in cold water) for 15 minutes.

HEALTH USE: Nutritionally, dandelion is a rich source of vitamins A to E, plus inositol, lecithin, and minerals such as iron, magnesium, manganese, calcium, copper, silicon, sodium, phosphorus, and zinc. Dandelion leaf is noted to be one of the richest vegetable sources of beta-carotene. Dandelion's name "pissenlit" (originating from the French *pisser en lit*—"to pee in bed") indicates use of leaves as a potassium-sparing diuretic. When my husband was released from the hospital after a surgery and suffered extreme edema late that night (while we were far away from medical help or phone contact), a strong dandelion leaf tea provided profound relief. Dandelion root could well be Alaska's number one herbal helper for livers compromised by overindulgence of alcohol or fats. A scientific paper published by an Iraq university states, "Dandelion improves the function of liver, pancreas and stomach. It is used to treat anemia, cirrhosis of the liver, hepatitis and rheumatism. An active dandelion constituent reduces serum cholesterol and triglycerides because it intensifies bile secretion." In addition, dandelion has been considered a key antidiabetic plant because of its antihyperglycemic, anti-inflammatory, and antioxidative properties.

OTHER: Dandelion flower massage oil provides soothing relief for muscular tension. To make, gently heat flowers in almond oil in the top of a double boiler until a rich color results.

CAUTION: Avoid harvesting in sprayed areas. Be certain to distinguish dandelions from other yellow composites like "false dandelion" (*Hypochaeris*), which is characterized by yellow composite "dandelion-like" flowers borne on long branched stems and hairy basal leaves.

BEDSTRAW
Galium species
Madder family (Rubiaceae)

Bedstraw is another free ranger, adapting to diverse conditions of seashores, moist woods, gardens, and mossy wet places. *Galiums* have square stems and leaves arranged in whorls. The small flowers have 4 white petals that vary with species from sparse to dense clusters. Fruits may be paired or singular, smooth, bristly, or covered with hooked hairs. Alaskan species include northern bedstraw (*G. boreale*), sweet-scented bedstraw (*G. triflorum*), the weak-stemmed sticks-to-everything cleavers (*G. aparine*, above), and others.

DERIVATION OF NAME: The botanical name *Galium* is from Greek gala, meaning "milk." Bedstraws were traditionally used as rennet for coagulating milk in cheesemaking.

OTHER NAMES: goosegrass, stick-a-back, maid's hair, Our Lady's bedstraw, *ts'ał t'áwsgad* (Haida, "its-seeds-stick-to-you").

RANGE: Throughout Alaska, except for the extreme north Arctic.

HARVESTING DIRECTIONS: Collect spring leaves and stems before flowering. Harvest the fruits in late summer.

FOOD USE: Only smooth-stemmed varieties can be eaten raw. Use in green drinks, pesto, herbal vinegars, and rice dishes. To improve texture, steam greens lightly. The flowering herbs can substitute for green tea. The fruits (which look like 2 little balls stuck together) are related to coffee. United Kingdom forager Rachel Lambert recommends roasting cleavers fruits for 40 minutes at 275°F (140°C) until a rich coffee aroma results. Grind and then brew in a French press or, for a stronger flavor, decoct (simmer) the brew.

HEALTH USE: Herbalists advocate cleavers (*G. aparine*) as a tea and a tincture to treat lymphatic system and urinary tract imbalances. *Galium* juice, ointment, and poultices soothe burns and skin ulcers. Dena'ina Athabascans apply *G. boreale*, which they call *ts'elveni vets'elq'a* "wormwood's partner," as a hot pack for aches and pains. In the Ukraine, clinical trials demonstrated that *Galium* species have "low toxicity and a broad spectrum of antimicrobial activity." An Iraqi medical journal states that "Previous pharmacological studies showed that *Galium aparine* extracts possessed antimicrobial, anticancer and hepatoprotective effects."

OTHER: Scottish forager Monica Wilde thoroughly describes the process of using bedstraw in cheese in her blog, monicawilde.com. Campers can use the tangled mats of cleavers as strainers for wilderness tea.

CAUTION: Some individuals experience contact dermatitis with cleavers.

WILLOW
Salix species
Willow family (Salicaceae)

Moose and humans enjoy eating willow, but both are quite particular about the species they consume. A mutual favorite is *surah* (*Salix pulchra*); its long, narrow leaves are smooth on both sides, darker green above, with margins that are generally smooth. The young leaves produce a refreshing aftertaste. *Surah* ranges from the northern Panhandle to Kodiak and the Alaska Peninsula and across the Interior to Utqiagvik (formerly Barrow). The sweet, inner bark and peeled shoots of the feltleaf willow, *Salix alaxensis*, are favored by the Iñupiat. Nearly 60 Alaskan species collectively range into all parts of the state. The diminutive, round-leaved netted willow (*S. reticulata*) roams from tundra to mountains. Dwarf *S. ovalifolia* favors salt marshes of the Arctic. The long-beaked willow *S. depressa* prefers woods and can grow to 30 feet tall.

DERIVATION OF NAME: *Salix* is the classical Latin name for willow.

OTHER NAMES: osier, pussy willow, *sura* (Iñupiat) *tsuaq* (Yup'ik), *ch'áal'* (Tlingit).

RANGE: Throughout Alaska.

HARVESTING DIRECTIONS: Pick *surah* leaves in early spring, when bright green and sweet. Peel shoots of the feltleaf willow, keeping the tasty green cambium (inner bark) and discarding the outer bark and woody core.

FOOD USE: Nibble *surah* leaves as a snack or add to salads. Their mild leaves blend well in soups and casseroles. Ferment with cabbage as sauerkraut. A mere 1 ounce of willow leaf fulfills your daily requirement for vitamin A and 89% of your vitamin C. The green cambium can be dried and ground as a flour substitute. (Such use is uncommon unless in survival situations).

HEALTH USE: Willow introduces foragers to the scientific discipline of organoleptic testing. This methodology uses human senses for evaluating substances. Foragers who taste willows will quickly differentiate those that are palatable for food purposes versus those high in the anti-inflammatory salicin. The rule of thumb is the more "yuck!" the willow tastes, the higher in pain-relieving compounds. Though slower acting than aspirin, willows offer advantages of longer-lasting pain relief, no stomach bleeding, and no effect on blood platelets. If troubled by headache in the wild, chew willow inner bark and leaves. Alternately, simmer the chopped inner bark in water, and sip the dark brew. For insect stings and bites, mash willow leaves and place the pulp on the irritated area. Use bark decoctions as an antiseptic wash for wilderness wounds. European herbalists use willow for treating colds, flu, fevers, headaches, and arthritis. Similar use is shared by Natives throughout Alaska. In addition, Iñupiat use willow bark ash for soothing burns. Yup'ik chewed willow bark and leaves for mouth sores.

OTHER: Soak sore feet in a willow footbath. Use leafy branches as a switch in the sauna to stimulate circulation. Use willow stems in basketry. To banish winter blues, place twigs in a vase of water and celebrate the pussy willow's promise of spring.

CAUTION: Individuals with sensitivity to aspirin are typically warned not to ingest salicin-containing plants (willow, poplar, birch). The American Botanical Council, however, points out that "the salicylates in willow metabolize differently than aspirin (acetylsalicylic acid)." Though it's possible for salicylate interactions to arise, studies do not indicate this potential toxicity. If in doubt if willow is right for you, check with your health care provider.

RHODIOLA
Sedum rosea, subspecies *integrifolia,* aka *Rhodiola rosea*
Stonecrop family (Crassulaceae)

I cultivated roseroot in my Kachemak Bay garden decades before the boon of commercial Alaskan cultivation. My start was finding a clump of *Sedum rosea* nesting in an eroded clump of earth, about to wash out to sea. I added it to my herb garden, envisioning a steady source of spring food; it thrived despite my total ignorance of its needs. Since the 1990s, research on this plant has expanded, as has cultivation knowhow. Today, it is marketed as Rhodiola. The name "roseroot" hints at the aroma of the rootstalk. The fleshy blue-gray leaves are spoon-shaped and overlap in a spiral fashion. The early blooming flowers sit at the top of the stem.

DERIVATION OF NAME: *Sedum* is from the Latin "to sit"; *rosea* means "rose."

OTHER NAMES: roseroot, Arctic root, hen and chickens.

RANGE: Moist rocky places, and alpine slopes throughout Alaska.

HARVESTING DIRECTIONS: For food use, leaves are most prime before flowers but can be used throughout the summer to extend food supplies. For health use, roots are harvested autumn or early spring.

FOOD USE: Eat Rhodiola leaves raw, in salads and coleslaws, or steam as a potherb. Add to immune support soup, with seaweed, miso, wild chives, and shitake. Try a Rhodiola relish or salsa. Include Rhodiola in egg dishes, stir-fries, and casseroles. Anore Jones reports that St. Lawrence Iñupiat ferment the rootstalks in water, adding successive layers every few weeks until the barrel is full. When it tastes sour, it is eaten with seal oil or blubber; the remainder is frozen for winter use.

HEALTH USE: The greens are high in vitamins A and C. Dena'ina Athabascans use leaves and rootstalks as tea for colds, sore-throat gargles, and eyewashes; the mashed rhizome is a poultice for cuts. Dr. Robert Fortuine documented use of roseroot flowers by Nelson and Nunivak Island Yup'ik for treatment of tuberculosis. Herbalists classify *Rhodiola* as an adaptogen, an herb that helps the body adapt to stress and anxiety. A Swedish clinical trial confirmed that standardized extracts exhibited a positive effect on fatigue levels and stress-related cognitive function, increasing attention and endurance.

OTHER: In 2009, Dr. Petra Illig successfully trialed 100,000 Rhodiola seedlings in Anchorage. But be warned: Illig writes that "it takes *Rhodiola rosea* at least 5 years in carefully tended fields to reach the state of maturity required to produce potent rosavin and saldiroside levels at the same concentrations as is found in mature wild roots." Also, Rhodiola prefers cold winters and cool summers; thus, ongoing global warming could potentially have adverse effects on future success. "At present Rhodiola," points out Smithsonian.com "already fetches a higher price per acre than other crops, such as potatoes."

CAUTION: An American Botanical Council HerbGram concludes that though *R. rosea* has very few side effects with most users finding it improves their mood, energy level, and mental clarity, it should be used with caution by individuals who tend to be anxious, jittery, or agitated. Also, those with bipolar disorder with a tendency to have manic periods may find it overly stimulating.

SAXIFRAGE
Saxifraga species
Saxifrage family (Saxifragaceae)

The *Saxifraga* genus is a large one and can be confusing, but fortunately it's forager friendly. My preferred species for eating is brook saxifrage, *Saxifraga punctata*, which has smooth, kidney-shaped leaves with toothed margins and a spike of white flowers; as the name indicates, it is common along streams. Leaves grow singly on basal stems. Inuit people eat flowers and petals of *aupilaktunnguat*, purple mountain saxifrage, *Saxifraga oppositifolia*. Saxifrage flower colors vary from white to yellow to violet red. Look closely and you'll note 5 petals with 10 stamens with a very visible ovary in the center. Seed capsules are red. A plant sometimes mistaken for brook saxifrage is mist maiden (*Romanzoffia*); leaves are similar in shape and equally edible.

DERIVATION OF NAME: *Saxifraga* is from the Latin *saxum*, "rock," and *frango*, "to break." Saxifrage thrives in rock fissures, creating the illusion it breaks rocks. Another theory of derivation relates to saxifrage's ancient use in dissolving urinary stones.

OTHER NAMES: brook saxifrage, salad greens, deer tongue.

RANGE: Throughout Alaska. Habitats vary with species from moist places to rockslides to rock crevices to bogs.

HARVESTING DIRECTIONS: Leaves are prime before flowers appear, but for camping purposes can be harvested all summer.

FOOD USE: Add saxifrage leaves to salads or stir-fries. Though they won't win kudos on *MasterChef* due to their rather bland flavor, they're a good source of vitamins A and C and can be dressed up with more flavorsome greens or sauces. Use in soups, quiche, spanakopita, and casseroles.

HEALTH USE: Bog saxifrage, *Saxifraga hirculus*, is a tufted species with short runners and yellow petals. It ranges in Alaska as well as in Pakistan, where the plant's decoction is given in fever, diarrhea, cough, chest complaints and pulmonary disorders. Spanish *Saxifraga* species are used as poultices for bruises, bites and boils. If camping in the alpine and needing relief from mosquito bites, a poultice of mashed saxifrage leaf could be worth trying.

OTHER: In the UK, University of Cambridge scientists have discovered the rare mineral vaterite in the "crust" that forms on various alpine saxifrage species. Vaterite is of significant interest to the pharmaceutical industry as a superior carrier for medications and as an ingredient in cements for orthopedic surgery.

Sea & Sandy Shores

Alaska and its islands offer 33,904 miles of coastal foraging opportunities. The proverb "when the tide is out, the table is set" doesn't apply for every single beach, of course, but I've always quipped that if I had to be stranded somewhere in Alaska, may it please be by the sea.

This section includes gravel beaches, tidal marshes, and rocky intertidal and subtidal zones. Here, many coastal plants including beach greens and goosetongue have developed fleshy stems and leaves to withstand desiccation in this salt-kissed environment. And algae, such as bladderwrack, have adapted to the extreme contrast between being immersed in sea and then exposed on land to glaring sun.

The Alaska Department of Fish and Game allows kelp harvesting along most of Alaska's coast for personal, non-commercial use. Fish and Game classifies most of Alaska's coast as a "subsistence use area." Within such areas, seaweed may be harvested without a sport fishing license or harvest limit. Exceptions to this rule, at time of publication, include Cook Inlet. Check with your regional office for current local rules.

Note that within the beach plants, the algae are organized progressively from ocean to shore. First is bull kelp, which exists in the ocean at all times. Progressing shoreward, the algae are arranged in the "biobands" where they occur. As the tide drops, the dark brown bladed algae (including ribbon kelp) are exposed, then the red algae (dulse and nori), followed by the green (sea lettuce). Closest to shore is the brown rockweed, bladderwrack.

Algae are particularly forager friendly, with only one known "toxic" kelp in Alaskan waters. A nibble of the inedible hairy unappetising Desmarestia won't harm you, and the flavor of this "acid kelp" will discourage you from eating more.

The remaining beach plants are arranged in alphabetical order by common name.

BULL KELP
Nereocystis luetkeana
Laminariaceae (family)
Brown algae (division Phaeophyta)

The kelp beds common along southern Alaska coasts are a hazard for boaters, who can foul their props in the tangles. But they are a favorite place for sea otters to park pups while mom fishes. Kelp blades grow to 10 feet long, and stipes (stems) can reach 100 to 175 feet in length in a single year. A branch-like holdfast attaches bull kelp to the seafloor. At the surface, an inflated bulb floats long, narrow blades.

DERIVATION OF NAME: The genus name is from the Greek *nereo*, "sea nymph," and *cystis*, "bladder;" *luetkeana* honors a Russian sea captain.

OTHER NAMES: bullwhip kelp, *meq'aq, gahnguq* (Yup'ik), *sú* (Tlingit), *tutł'ila* (Dena'ina, "water rope").

RANGE: Southeast Alaska to Kodiak and the Kenai Peninsula to the Aleutian Islands.

HARVESTING DIRECTIONS: Bull kelp is prime from April to June. Use a boat and hook to collect plants attached to the ocean floor. Just 1 or 2 can feed a family. If boatless, visit the beach at an ultra-minus tide, with waders, to retrieve one. Or check for freshly uprooted kelp. Avoid older beach drift (unless collecting just for garden mulch).

FOOD USE: Every part of kelp except the holdfast has edible applications. Munch on the blades raw for a "salty cabbage" snack. Wrap a salmon in the fresh kelp blades and cook on the campfire; serve the kelp as a vegetable. Blanch blades (as described in ribbon kelp) and use similarly as salad. Dry bull kelp blades and grind as a table seasoning. Or massage raw blades with olive oil, garlic, nutritional yeast, and spices and then dehydrate for "chips." I prefer to peel the stipe, then slice and use the raw rings atop pizza. Try marinating kelp rings in honey or syrup and then dehydrating; tasters guessed I was feeding them dry pineapple. Use stem, peeled or unpeeled, as you prefer, slice into rings, and pickle with your favorite recipe. My dear friend Marsha Million "French cut" kelp stems like string beans and canned for winter use. Stuff the kelp bulb with meat or vegetarian stuffing and bake.

HEALTH USE: The blades of bull kelp have a protein content twice that of the bulb and stipe, and appreciable quantities of calcium, potassium, and iron. Small amounts of seaweed daily are far better than large amounts occasionally. Herbalist Ryan Drum points out that in some individuals it may take a person "up to 4 months to produce dedicated enzymes to thoroughly digest dietary seaweeds." Drum emphasizes the importance of sufficient dietary iodine, the link between low iodine and hypothyroidism and goiter and how "eating 3-5 grams of most dried, unrinsed seaweeds will provide the RDA of 100–150 micrograms."

OTHER: Campers can soak sore feet in a kelp footbath. Entertain the whole family with a kelp horn—remove the end of the bulb and leave a 2-foot-long handle to blow into. Use kelp as a candle mold; fill kelp bulbs with a candlewick and hot wax; when the wax is set, discard the kelp.

CAUTION: If you experience hyperthyroidism, consult your doctor or clinical herbalist before use.

RIBBON KELP
Alaria species
Alariaceae (family)
Brown algae (division Phaeophyta)

I'm often asked which plant is my favorite, and the answer varies with place and season. Put me on an Alaskan beach in spring, and I'll quickly be munching on my "favorite," ribbon kelp. It's easy to recognize with its smooth, olive-green to brown blade, 3 to 9 feet long, and its distinctive flattened midrib. At the base, between the holdfast and the main blade, are 2 opposite rows of smaller, wing-like blades.

DERIVATION OF NAME: *Alaria* is Latin for winged.

OTHER NAMES: winged kelp, *wakame.*

RANGE: Southeast Alaska to the Bering Sea.

HARVESTING DIRECTIONS: Ribbon kelp is prime from April to June. Clip ribbon kelp above the sporophylls (i.e. wing-like lower blades) to allow the algae to regenerate. The smaller first-year fronds are most tender and tasty. Discard any tattered edges of the main blade. Pick clean of shells. To dry for year-round use, hang across lines or poles. Separate the fronds well for good air ventilation. When fully dry, store in jars in a cool dark place.

FOOD USE: Nibble ribbon kelp fresh. The central midrib has a delightful crunchy texture and mild flavor and can be used as a water chestnut substitute. I love dried ribbon kelp toasted in a skillet with olive oil, sunflower, and pumpkin seeds, and seasonings as a salad topping. Add fresh or dried ribbon kelp to miso soups. My favorite beach salad is blanched ribbon kelp, sliced and sautéed in sesame oil with garlic, carrots, and ginger. The brown seaweed turns a brilliant kelly green when blanched! Add a teaspoon of the powdered dry alga to breads and baked goods to increase nutritional value. Note: the sporophylls are considered a delicacy raw or cooked; harvest selectively to ensure ongoing supply.

HEALTH USE: Ribbon kelp is an ideal snack food—low in calories, high in flavor and nutrients, especially protein, calcium, phosphorus, potassium, magnesium, and B vitamins. Ribbon kelp contains alginic acid, which binds radioactive strontium in the intestines and aids its excretion from the body. As a tonic tea (or food), it strengthens body systems, including reproductive organs and skin. Clinical studies by Japanese researchers Okai and others indicate that the epidemiologic evidence for seaweed as a chemopreventive food is very compelling. Although daily seaweed consumption is not uniform, even in Japan, people in Okinawa consume more seaweed and have the lowest cancer incidence, mortality, and longest life spans. American researcher Jane Teas notes that a vast number of seaweed studies on animals have been done, all of which confirm the nontoxic effects of seaweed on normal cells and in healthy animals, and cytotoxic effects against cancer cells and tumors.

OTHER: For a home spa treatment, take a ribbon kelp bath. For a facial, blend white cosmetic-grade clay with powdered ribbon kelp and a bit of honey. Ribbon kelp is available for free from Alaskan beaches and can also be bought in natural-food stores as *Alaria* or *wakame.* Note that *wakame* is also a common name for *Undaria pinnatifida,* a seaweed considered globally invasive.

DULSE
Palmaria species (formerly *Rhodymenia*)
Palmariaceae (family)
Red algae (division Rhodophyta)

If you're sampling sea vegetables for the first time, try dulse. Dulse "potato chips" (directions in Food Use) are popular with kids and adults because of their salty taste and crunchy texture. Look for purple-red blades, 4 to 12 inches in length. Alaska has 3 dulse species: *Palmaria hecatensis* (formerly *Palmaria palmata*) whose use has been recorded in Iceland since the year 960, *P. mollis* (also formerly *P. palmata*), and the stiffer, narrower, frilly *P. callophylloides*. All are safe.

DERIVATION OF NAME: *Palmaria* is from the Latin for "palm of the hand," referring to the shape of the algae blades.

OTHER NAMES: red ribbon, red kale, dillisk, Nepture's girdle, waterleaf.

RANGE: Southeast Alaska to Kodiak, and the Gulf of Alaska to the Aleutian Islands.

HARVESTING DIRECTIONS: Clip fronds above the holdfast, pick clean of shells, and rinse in ocean water. Dulse is prime from April to June.

FOOD USE: Nibble dulse fresh from the beach. Raw dulse is somewhat rubbery. For dulse "potato chips," quickly stir-fry dry dulse in a few drops of olive or sesame oil, stirring constantly until crisp (be careful not to burn the dulse). Try a DLT sandwich: dulse chips (instead of bacon) with lettuce and tomato. Dry and grind dulse as a seasoning for potatoes or rice. If you are cooking beans or lentils, add some dulse to enhance their digestibility.

HEALTH USE: Dulse is highest in protein (21%) when harvested late winter to spring. It contains essential amino acids and omega-3 and omega-6 oils. Those with sensitivity to dairy may be interested to note that compared to milk, 100 g of dulse contains more calcium (148 mg versus 115 mg), more magnesium (97 mg versus 11 mg), and more potassium (1,169 mg versus 140 mg). For vegans, dulse is a source of B12. Dulse has both antioxidant and antimicrobial properties. Add dulse to salves for cold sores, sunburn, and general cuts and scrapes.

OTHER: I enjoy a rejuvenating dulse bath after airline travel; during long journeys, I consider sea vegetables an essential snack. Use of dulse and our subsistence right to harvest was recorded in a 12th-century Iceland law book; this declared it legal to collect and eat dulse when on another man's property.

CAUTION: Due to iodine content in algae, consult your doctor if on thyroid medicines.

NORI
Porphyra species
Bangiaceae (family)
Red algae (division Rhodophyta)

If you've ever eaten sushi, you've eaten nori. Nori ranges globally on rocky shores from Alaska to New Zealand (where it is commonly called "karengo"). In the ocean, nori resembles a long, transparent rubber glove. The linear blades are 1 cell thick and up to 1 foot in length, attached to rocks by a small holdfast. On hot days, at low tide, nori looks like a black smear on exposed rocks, but don't let its unappetizing appearance deceive you. This favorite of sea vegetables commands a premium price, and for good reason. Alaska has a dozen *Porphyra* species (photos can be seen on the *Seaweeds of Alaska* website, seaweedsofalaska.com). Though classed as a red alga, colors are variable with species from greenish to brown to reddish. All are safe for foragers.

DERIVATION OF NAME: *Porphyra* is from the Greek for "purple."

OTHER NAMES: laver, black seaweed, purple laver, *tsaqałqaq* (Yup'ik).

RANGE: Southeast Alaska to the Aleutians to the Bering Sea.

HARVESTING DIRECTIONS: Collect nori at low tide, snipping the plant an inch above the holdfast. Rinse with ocean water to remove sand and grit. To ensure regeneration, avoid yanking up the entire plant.

FOOD USE: Called "black seaweed" in Southeast Alaska, *Porphyra* is an important subsistence and trade item for Tlingit, Haida, and Tsimshian people. Dorothy Garza in *Common Edible Seaweeds in the Gulf of Alaska* recommends drying outdoors on a sunny breezy day, taking care to keep separating the bundles as they dry. They are then finished by dry roasting at 175°F for 10 to 20 minutes. They are a fantastic snack! *Food and Wine* magazine suggests such trendy *Porphyra* delicacies as fish on fried nori crackers, nori vinaigrette, Japanese popcorn, nori-granola, and nori-crusted sirloin. I'm salivating dreaming of nori-crusted silver salmon, potatoes with nori gratin, nori chips, nori and beetroot veggie burgers, and nori and seafood chowder. My favorite wilderness "mock oysters" were fresh nori, rolled into a ball, dipped in an egg-milk mixture, then dusted with flour and ground oats and seasonings, and fried.

HEALTH USE: According to the Food and Agriculture Organization, nori is "among the most nutritious seaweeds, with a protein content of 30–50%, and about 75% of that is digestible. Sugars are low (0.1%), and the vitamin content very high, with significant amounts of vitamins A, B1, B2, B6, B12, C, niacin and folic acid." Researchers McHugh and Dennis add that vitamin C shelf life is short in the dried products. Alaskans are fortunate in having ready access to fresh and freshly dried nori.

OTHER: To make seaweed wrappers for sushi, nori is harvested, dried, minced, and, in a process somewhat akin to papermaking, processed into flat sheets. Japan alone produces an average of 400,000 tons (wet weight) of *Porphyra* per year, which is processed into approximately 10 billion nori sheets with a market value of over $1.5 billion.

CAUTION: Check with your doctor about recommended consumption if taking thyroid medication or blood thinners.

SEA LETTUCE
Ulva lactuca
Ulvaceae (family)
Green algae (division Chlorophyta)

Sea lettuce is a globetrotter ranging along Arctic Alaska coasts to sunny California, China, Russia, and New Zealand. Go to your favorite beach at low tide and look for paper-thin, green, transparent blades growing on rocks. These broad blades can grow to 2 feet in length, though the Alaskan specimens I've found have always been less than a foot. Edges may be ruffled, resembling frilled lettuce on a rock; sea lettuce may bear tiny holes in their blades. (Botanists used to consider *Ulva fenestra*, the sea lettuce bearing holes or "windows" in its blades, a separate species from the common *Ulva lactuca*, but now tend to lump them as one.)

DERIVATION OF NAME: *Ulva* is a classical Latin name first used by Virgil; *lactuca* means "lettuce."

OTHER NAMES: water lettuce, green laver, *tātsch* (Tlingit).

RANGE: Southeast Alaska to the Aleutians and Kamchatka Peninsula.

HARVESTING DIRECTIONS: Gather sea lettuce in spring to early summer, when blades are bright green. Pick free of shells. Remove areas bruised by the tide and rocks. If sandy, rinse with cool saltwater. (If you see sea lettuce with white edges, this indicates that the mature plant has released its free-swimming reproductive cells. Harvest early in the summer before this occurs.)

FOOD USE: Chop young sea lettuce for salads or boil briefly (1 to 2 minutes) as a potherb. Add to salmon dishes, and noodle or stir-fry meals. Sea lettuce is my favorite powdered sea vegetable seasoning. Its bright green color and salty flavor make it a colorful and tasty garnish for rice, and even popcorn. Students in my classes have substituted sea lettuce for nori in wraps for sushi. A blog by forager Louise Fawcett details step by step a method for making your own sea lettuce wraps: seaweedrecipes.co.nz/make-your-own-seaweed-wraps-its-easy.

HEALTH USE: Sea lettuce contains protein, the alphabet of vitamins from A to K (including B12), and bone-strengthening calcium, magnesium, and other trace minerals. Beach campers can apply sea lettuce as a poultice for soothing windburn or sunburn. In France, a double-blind randomized placebo-controlled trial showed that taking a sea lettuce water extract daily for 3 months continued to significantly improve depressed patients with anhedonia (the inability to experience pleasure in normally pleasurable activities). Authors Allaert, Demais, and Collén underscored the high potential for using sea lettuce in everyday clinical care "particularly as it would avoid the undesirable effects of medicinal drugs currently used." They emphasized that "depressive symptoms continued to improve in subjects taking the water-soluble Ulva L.L. extract."

OTHER: To dry sea lettuce, place on a hot sunny windowsill or in a vegetable/herb drier.

CAUTION: As always, harvest only in clean areas free of contaminants. In France in 2009, 2,000 tons of sea lettuce washed up on Brittany beaches, emitting toxic hydrogen sulfide gas during decomposition. Sea lettuce is the algae most linked to "green tides" caused by human agricultural activities and sewage outfalls. Though previously viewed as problematic, science is revealing the potential of algae blooms to produce renewable gaseous fuel. Dried, washed, macerated *Ulva* from an estuary algal bloom was shown, in a PubMed study, to be sufficient to provide fuel for 264 cars on a year-round basis.

BLADDERWRACK
Fucus species
Fucaceae (family)
Brown algae (division Phaeophyta)

Bladderwrack is an easy-to-recognize sea vegetable, found attached to rocks along ocean shores of Alaska and most of the world. The olive-brown blades, which grow to 18 inches in length, divide in twos and have prominent midribs. The distinctive inflated tips are mucilaginous. These bladders contain the male and female gametes (eggs and sperm) that have propagated these algae for over 400 million years.

DERIVATION OF NAME: The botanical name *Fucus* is from the Greek *phykos*, meaning "seaweed."

OTHER NAMES: rockweed, popweed, old man's firecrackers, *caritet* (Alutiiq).

RANGE: Southeast Alaska to the Chukchi Sea.

HARVESTING DIRECTIONS: Collect the inflated tips and tender ends of fronds from late winter to early summer. Clip above the small disc-like holdfast that anchors the sea vegetable to rocks. Remove any snails or debris. Rinse in ocean water.

FOOD USE: Nibble bladderwrack raw on beach hikes. Steam *Fucus* with clams or mussels to heighten flavors. Add fresh chopped tips to pasta sauce as a thickener. Try popweed chips; rub bladderwrack tips thoroughly with a blend of olive oil, tamari or coconut aminos, nutritional yeast, and seasonings of choice, and then dehydrate until crisp. Pour boiling water over 1 teaspoon fresh or sun-dried *Fucus* for a tasty tea; add mint, nettles, lemon, or other flavorings as desired. Use fresh or dry bladderwrack in soup starter or fish broth. Sauté bladderwrack with fresh onions and ginger, a dash of sweet and sour sauce, sesame seeds, and goosetongue. Kodiak Alutiiq call bladderwrack *caritet* and eat it raw, dipped in oil or with sea urchin eggs.

HEALTH USE: If you get burned while cooking on your beach campfire, break open a *Fucus* bladder for its soothing aloe-like gel. Soak your tired feet in a bladderwrack footbath. Bladderwrack contains the alphabet of vitamins (A to E, as well as K), and a complex array of minerals and trace elements. Clinical studies at McGill University confirm that sodium alginate in *Fucus* and other brown algae binds with radioactive strontium 90 in the intestines, thus causing it (as well as heavy metals) to be eliminated from the body. Another clinical trial notes the ability of *Fucus* to lower cholesterol levels and to reduce risk of estrogen-related cancers.

OTHER: Burn dry bladderwrack with alder to smoke salmon. Nourish your beds of potatoes and cabbage with potash-rich *Fucus*. In Ireland in the 1900s, there were some 300 seaweed bathhouses popular for relieving stress and tired muscles; indulge in the seaweed spa in your very own home. Finish off with a bladderwrack hair rinse.

CAUTION: Due to the mucilage in bladderwrack tips, bladderwrack can have a laxative effect. Harvest only in uncontaminated waters. Consult your doctor concerning use if you have any type of thyroid imbalance or are taking any blood-thinner medication.

BEACH GREENS
Honckenya peploides, aka *Arenaria peploides*
Pink family (Carophyllaceae)

Beach greens are a stunning example of the power of regeneration of plants. From the brown, seemingly winter-killed trailing stems emerge bright green shoots packed with vitamins A and C. The trailing stems grow to 2 feet long, with smooth, fleshy, sharply pointed leaves in opposite arrangement. The small greenish-white flowers are followed by globular seed capsules.

DERIVATION OF NAME: *Honckenya* honors 18th-century German botanist Gerhard Honckeny; *peploides*, from the Greek word for a cloak, describes the way the leaves wrap the stems and nearly hide the flowers.

OTHER NAMES: scurvygrass, sea purslane.

RANGE: Sandy shores from Southeast Alaska to the Arctic.

HARVESTING DIRECTIONS: Young leaves and shoots are prime before flowers appear; wash well to remove the grit and sand that may be trapped by the cloak-like leaves.

FOOD USE: Beach greens are an important subsistence food in coastal Native villages and have been traditionally fermented for year-round use. Forager Corinne Conlon, writing in the *Juneau Empire*, recommends that when starting to cook with any new edible, contemplate its resemblance to plants you already use. Noting that beach green's flavor is similar to that "of a Napa cabbage mixed with a sweet pea," Corinne used beach greens in her favorite Indian kofta cabbage dish. I include young leaves in seaside stir-fries, soups, and salads. Process into pesto for lasagna. Leaf flavor intensifies after flowering, but the plant can still be quite useful if marinated with oil and vinegar, added to curries, or blended lightly into casseroles with milder greens like goosetongue. Experiment with sprouting the seeds for winter salads, or toast seeds lightly in a skillet and add to homemade crackers or as a garnish on rice. I also like adding young beach greens to fermented cabbage sauerkraut. Or try making Iñupiat style *atchaaqtuk*, fermented beach greens. Directions are detailed in Anore Jones's *Plants That We Eat: Nauriat Nigiñaqtuat*.

HEALTH USE: The humble circumpolar beach greens (along with Alaska's spoonwort mustard *Cochlearia*) have saved lives of many a crew due to their high vitamin C content. According to scholar James Beaglehole, all seafarers were affected by scurvy, "a greater obstacle to long-distance navigation than all other factors, human or technical." Symptoms of exhaustion, depression, night terrors, swollen joints, and suppurating sores all followed from the mere fact of lacking greens in the diet.

OTHER: Beach greens can form a comfortable camping mat for your sleeping bag, but be aware that they are a favorite food of black bears. If camping near river mouths, beach greens can actually be covered by the rising tide—a fact I learned the hard way!

BEACH PEA

Lathyrus maritimus, aka *L. japonicus maritimus*
Pea family (Fabaceae), Pea subfamily (Faboideae), Pea tribe (Fabeae)

Beach pea is specific to gravel beaches, bears a typical reddish-pink to purple "pea" blossom with wings and keel, has smooth unjointed pods, and has tendrils at the end of the stem. Beach peas, when properly identified and eaten in moderation, are safe and nourishing. Note that in some plant guides, beach peas are listed as toxic, a reputation not fully deserved. It is true that the grass pea *Lathyrus sativus*, of Bangladesh and Ethiopia, when consumed as 30% of a famished person's caloric intake for 3 to 4 months, can trigger lathyrism. Lathyrism is a degenerative neuromuscular disease characterized by partial or total paralysis. However, if the peas are well cooked and part of a normal, balanced diet, the problem does not occur.

DERIVATION OF NAME: *Lathyrus* is from the Greek *la thoursos*, meaning "something exciting," (reputed to be related to aphrodisiacal qualities); *maritimus* indicates the plant's habitat.

OTHER NAMES: purple beach pea, seaside pea, raven's canoe.

RANGE: Southeast Alaska shores to Icy Cape in the Chukchi Sea.

HARVESTING DIRECTIONS: Harvest young shoots when under 10 inches high. Pick "snowpea" pods when bright green. Shell the peas when pods mature and peas are still green.

FOOD USE: The purple flowers are a tasty and edible garnish to salads and cooked dishes. Steam or stir-fry young beach pea greens. Simmer young "snow pea" pods 3 to 5 minutes till tender. The green peas, removed from green summer pods, are a tasty vegetable.

HEALTH USE: Beach peas are a high-protein food source. Sixteenth-century Chinese herbalists considered beach pea particularly strengthening to the intestinal tract and urinary tract. A study on *Lathyrus* species done by Turkish, Italian, and Spanish researchers noted their antioxidant values and recommend further studies on *Lathyrus* species "for developing novel health-promoting agents by pharmaceutical and nutraceutical industries."

OTHER: Note that the pea family is one where some genera have both edible and inedible species (for example, *Hedysarum*, detailed in *Discovering Wild Plants*). The only *Lathyrus* species I personally have experienced is the common beach pea, *L. maritimus*. I've always taken great care to differentiate it from marsh pea, aka marsh vetchling, *Lathyrus palustris*, which is common in swampy ground. Marsh pea has butterfly-shaped leaves (stipules) at the base of its branched stems, whereas beach pea has broad stipules. I always warned students that if they ate the pea with the butterfly leaves, they might "fly" to the next world. I may be exaggerating, but the pea family deserves respect and caution.

CAUTION: If in a survival situation, do not subsist solely on any *Lathyrus* species. Abide by the wisdom of veteran forager Hank Shaw, author of the blog *Hunter, Angler, Gardener, Cook*, who has been eating beach peas a dozen or so times a year for the past 40 years. Hank believes that wild peas highlight one of the defining features of our human biology: "We *Homo sapiens* are designed, over a million years of experience in nature, to eat a little of a lot, not a lot of a little."

GLASSWORT
Salicornia species
Amaranth family (Amaranthaceae),
Pickleweed subfamily (Salicornioideae)

I first ate glasswort while camping in the Florida Keys and was delighted to rediscover it on Alaskan beaches. This salty "pickleplant" (sold in gourmet restaurants as sea asparagus or sea beans) is a globetrotter, establishing roots from North America to South Africa to Eurasia. Its common name varies with location, my favorite being the Quebec *titines de souris* (mouse tits). Alaskan species are generally 2 to 6 inches in height. The fleshy stems are jointed and may vary in hue from green to red. Flowers are minute, in groups of 3, hidden in the joints.

DERIVATION OF NAME: *Salicornia* translates as "salty horn," describing both the taste and the shape of the herb.

OTHER NAMES: pickleweed, sea asparagus, sea beans.

RANGE: Southeast Alaska and Kenai Peninsula to Anchorage.

HARVESTING DIRECTIONS: Harvest tender green-colored glasswort stems. Harvest selectively, and avoid disrupting roots so that the p atch will continue in abundance. Once the plants turn red, they are too old to harvest.

FOOD USE: Add glasswort to green salads, cold bean salads, and chowder. Steam as a potherb and drizzle with butter or garlic-sesame sauce. While camping, stuff a salmon with glasswort, wrap in kelp blades, and bake on the coals. Pickle glasswort or add to vegetable ferments. Later in the season, mature plants, if still green, can be steamed and eaten similarly to a globe artichoke bud. Dip in butter or curry mayonnaise and then drag the stems between your teeth to remove the tender portions.

HEALTH USE: In clinical studies on a Tunisian *Salicornia* species, glasswort exhibited antioxidant and antibacterial activities. Patel's study, published in Biotech, show that other species also demonstrate "immunomodulatory, lipid-lowering, antiproliferative, osteoprotective, and hypoglycemic properties." In Nicholas Culpeper's *Complete Herbal*, published in 1653, glasswort powder was recommended for drying running sores and alleviating ringworm. In 2014, a clinical trial in India studying *Salicornia's* effectiveness against fungal plant diseases confirmed that it "gave complete inhibition of the pathogen."

OTHER: Glasswort is an ingredient in a Korean rice wine, as well as *Salicornia* "ocean gin" by Blanc. It is a popular vegetable in Southeast Alaska, and even sold in supermarkets. Experiments are being conducted in Saudi Arabia and Mexico in cultivating *Salicornia* as a source of biodiesel for jet fuel. Traditionally, glasswort ashes were used in glassmaking and soapmaking. According to 16th-century English herbalist-physician John Gerard, burning the plants drives away serpents. It would be more useful in Alaska if it kept bears out of camp.

CAUTION: Glasswort can absorb toxins from oil spills or other environmental catastrophes. Though useful for bioremediation purposes, such plants would be unsuitable for consumption.

GOOSETONGUE

Plantago maritima
Plantain family (Plantaginaceae)

"Beach potato chips" is how I introduce young foragers to goosetongue. The greens have a refreshing salty taste popular with young and old. Physically, goosetongue has compact flower stalks (generally 6 to 12 inches in length); its yellowish stamens stick out and wave like hula dancers in the breeze. Leaves are long, narrow, and fleshy (see Caution on next page).

DERIVATION OF NAME: *Plantago* means "sole of the foot." *Maritima* means "maritime."

OTHER NAMES: beach plantain, seaside plantain, *sukhtéitl'* (Tlingit).

RANGE: Seacoasts and salt marshes from Southeast Alaska to the Aleutians and on the southern Seward Peninsula.

HARVESTING DIRECTIONS: Selectively pluck leaves from goosetongue clusters. For conservation purposes, do not take the entire plant. Be mindful not to disturb the roots while harvesting. As is typical with wild greens, goosetongue is prime before flowering from spring to early summer. However, even later in the season, I still actively seek it out for extra camping food; just be even more selective, choosing the youngest tender leaves growing in the center.

FOOD USE: Nibble raw goosetongue at the beach. Add chopped greens to salmon patties. Cook with clams or mussels. Steam greens as a potherb. Grind flower buds with a mortar and pestle; add lemon juice and olive oil for a tapenade (excellent on crackers). Add chopped leaves to chowders, salads, casseroles, spanakopita, and stir-fries. Blanch and freeze goosetongue for winter use. Toasted seeds can be used as a garnish.

HEALTH USE: In a Hungarian trial, goosetongue *P. maritima* was shown to have the highest antioxidant capacity of the 5 plantain species studied. Chew or mash goosetongue greens and apply to relieve itchy mosquito bites. All plantain seeds (including the non-Alaskan but commercially viable *P. psyllium*) swell if soaked in water overnight and can be used as an emergency bulk laxative when camping; drink with abundant water.

CAUTION: Goosetongue often grows with arrowgrass, a plant containing cyanide compounds in its leaves. I discovered arrowgrass decades ago, nibbling while collecting goosetongue and suddenly eating something which definitely lacked the distinct salty tang. Though a nibble will not harm you, you don't want to consume arrowgrass in quantity. Study the photos here and on page 180.

Goosetongue, in upper hand. Arrowgrass, in lower hand with watchband.

LOVAGE

Ligusticum scoticum, aka *L. scoticum,* subspecies *hulténii*
Parsley family (Apiaceae, formerly Umbelliferae)

Closely observe young lovage leaves and you'll typically note a characteristic crimson line as though a child has traced the margin with a red pen. Stems divide in 3, each bearing only 3 leaflets. Crush a leaf and notice its distinctive scent. Flowers are white to light pink in hue, arranged in umbels with 7 to 11 rays. Stems are reddish-purple at the base and grow to 2 feet high. To deepen your relationship with lovage and recognize it easily in all phases of growth, plant it in your herb garden. Though a plant of sandy, salty shores, it can also thrive in normal soil.

DERIVATION OF NAME: The genus name *Ligusticum scoticum* means "from Liguria," the area best known as the Italian Riviera. The species name refers to Scotland, and the subspecies name *hulténii* honors botanist Eric Hultén. The names indicate the many places this helpful plant roams.

OTHER NAMES: Scotch lovage, beach lovage, sea lovage, wild celery, *petrushki, bidrushga, pidrushga.* In some regions of Alaska, Russians were said to have introduced the Natives to the use of this plant (hence its Russian common names). Lovage is one of the many Alaskan plants of various genera dubbed "wild celery."

RANGE: Sandy beaches from Southeast Alaska north to Nome.

HARVESTING DIRECTIONS: Leaves are mildest and most tender before flowering; later in the season, part the herb and pick the tender bright green new growth in the center. Collect seeds in late summer.

FOOD USE: Chop spring lovage and mix with cream cheese as a spread; garnish with edible flowers for an attractive hors d'oeuvre. Infuse fresh young leaves in olive oil with garlic; use as salad dressing or as a marinade on halibut. Stuff a salmon with lovage before baking. Iñupiat eat young leaves raw with seal oil, often with meat or fish. Indigenous Alaskans commonly boil lovage with fish. Dry spring leaves as a spice. Add to soups, spaghetti sauce, and holiday stuffing. Even later summer leaves can be useable while camping if you cook in changes of water. Use seeds to season stews, breads, and sausage.

HEALTH USE: Lovage is high in vitamins A and C. Seeds are a traditional digestive aid and carminative tea (for expelling gas), as well as a flavoring agent for masking bitter medicines.

OTHER: Beach lovage *Ligusticum scoticum* is related to the Rocky Mountain "osha" *Ligusticum porteri*, a species noted for its antiviral properties. Do Alaskan specimens have similar properties and possibly even higher potency than those in the Lower 48 (just as Alaskan blueberries have higher antioxidant values)? More scientific research is needed on Alaskan specimens. To remove odors after handling garlic or fish, rub crushed lovage leaves between your palms. Add a large handful of lovage to a bucket of hot water for a fragrant and deodorizing sauna bath; though I can't guarantee your results, lovage baths are reputed to draw romance to your life.

CAUTION: Lovage bears the double-umbel flowers that characterize the celery/parsley family. This family contains prime edibles like lovage, as well as deadly toxics like poison water hemlock (*Cicuta* on page 176). Be 100% positive of what you are gathering!

ORACH
Atriplex species
Amaranth family (Amaranthaceae),
Goosefoot subfamily (Chenopodiaceae)

Grant me "naming power of plants" and I would transform "orach" to "beach spinach," for orach shares the goosefoot subfamily with garden spinach, as well as the cultivated "New Zealand spinach" (*Atriplex hortensis*), and the equally edible "lamb's quarter" (*Chenopodium album* on page 66). Orach seed develops within pairs of clasping leaves. Stem leaves are variable with *Atriplex* species, ranging from triangular to lanceolate-oblong. Lower leaves are opposite, upper leaves alternate.

DERIVATION OF NAME: *Atriplex* may come from the Latin roots for "dark" and "fold," describing the plant's clasping leaves. Another possible derivation is from the Greek word meaning "without nourishment," as the plants can grow in barren soils.

OTHER NAMES: saltbush, seascale, sea purslane.

RANGE: Coastally from Southeast Alaska to the Kenai Peninsula, Kodiak, and the Alaska Peninsula, and on the southern and northern Seward Peninsula.

HARVESTING DIRECTIONS: Selectively harvest tender shoots and leaves from spring through summer. Harvest seeds from late summer to early fall, making certain you leave plenty for these annual plants to regenerate.

FOOD USE: Scottish forager Mark Williams at Galloway Wild Foods extolls the flavor of *Atriplex*: "The tender young leaves, to my palate, are wonderfully sweet with nutty overtones and a hint of salt." Use leaves like spinach, raw in salads or added to campfire soups, egg scrambles, and stir-fries. Steam the greens as a side dish. Seeds are small and "fiddly" but could be used as a thickener like chia, or toasted lightly and sprinkled on rice or homemade crackers.

HEALTH USE: Leaves are a traditional poultice for wounds and insect bites. Research studies identify antiseptic and antibacterial properties in *Atriplex* species. More research is needed on Alaskan species; in Israel a gerbil that lacks access to *Atriplex halimus* is known to develop type 2 diabetes. *Alternative Medicine Review* notes that "The data on its use for type 2 diabetes in humans is limited to unpublished reports in which 3 g/day decreased blood glucose levels."

OTHER: The *Atriplex* genus has more than 250 species worldwide, in habitats ranging from the extremes of salty Arctic beaches to alkaline deserts. Animals grazing *Atriplex* species in high-selenium areas like South Dakota and Wyoming have experienced hoof wall deformities and lameness. Alaskan soils, on the other hand, tend to be low in selenium and are predicted to lessen even more with climate change.

OYSTERLEAF

Mertensia maritima
Borage family (Boraginaceae)

Oysterleaf is a plant so distinctive in blue-gray hue that you can often spot it at a distance! It has sometimes been called "vegetarian oyster" due to the unique leaf flavor. Interestingly, the American Chemical Society conducted research on *Mertensia maritima* constituents and found "after evaluation of freshly prepared reference samples, these compounds were confirmed to be reminiscent of the oyster-like marine notes perceived in the tasting of cut leaves." The bell-like blossoms are like chameleons changing from bright pink buds to blue (sometimes white) flowers. Stems trail on the ground and rise up at the tip.

DERIVATION OF NAME: *Mertensia* honors botanist Franz Karl Mertens; *maritima* refers to the habitat where this plant thrives.

OTHER NAME: oyster plant.

RANGE: Beaches from the northern Panhandle to the Arctic.

HARVESTING DIRECTIONS: In spring, selectively pick the basal leaves, making certain you leave plenty to allow the plant to thrive. Later in the season, harvest stem leaves and flowers. Though oysterleaf is most tender in May and June, leaves are palatable throughout the growing season.

FOOD USE: Nibble tender oysterleaf as a beach snack. Use as a base for salad or sandwich filling. Add to quiche and egg dishes, as well as chowders and soups. Flowers are an edible garnish.

HEALTH USE: In northern Europe, oysterleaf blended with fennel and honey water is a traditional remedy to soothe coughs. In a clinical study published in *Plant Cell Tissue and Organ Culture*, oysterleaf was found to contain rabdosiin and rosmarinic acid, as well as the skin-conditioning agent R-allantoin, representing "a potentially useful novel composition for skin protection." Add oysterleaf to your herbal lotions.

OTHER: Oysterleaf can vanish due to overgrazing by wandering stock. A Kachemak Bay friend fenced her seaside property to preserve oysterleaf, goosetongue, and other beach edibles for her dining pleasure. See chiming bells on page 102 for additional details on *Mertensia* species.

Gardens, Lawns & Disturbed Soils

Gardens, lawns, and disturbed soils are our most familiar habitats. The hard-packed soils of roadsides and driveways and the fertile soils of kempt fields are home to our most enthusiastic plant volunteers. Examples include global wanderers like plantain and dandelion who often feature as "poster children" on herbicide ads or even "invasive species" posters. I'd be delighted to see more and more of our backyard "weeds" on posters that celebrate their benefits. (Though Dandelion is a highly common lawn and garden 'weed', it is now placed in the free-range section as some Taraxacum species range to tundra, alpine, and scree slopes.)

CHICKWEED
Stellaria media
Pink family (Caryophyllaceae)

What gardener isn't familiar with chickweed—the prolific annual that volunteers so generously in cultivated soil? Take a close look and you'll discover a fine line of hairs running down one side of the stem only. The leaves are arranged in pairs on weak stems that often trail on the ground. Take a nibble, and you'll discover a very mild-flavored green. Look closely at the small white star-shaped flowers; you'll see that the 10 petals are actually 5 divided ones.

DERIVATION OF NAME: *Stellaria* refers to the star-like flowers; *media* means "intermediate."

OTHER NAMES: starwort, winterweed, stitchwort, skirt buttons, satin flower.

RANGE: Most areas of Alaska except north of the Brooks Range. Worldwide range extends from Asia, Africa, North and South America, and Europe to Australasia.

HARVESTING DIRECTIONS: Take scissors with you when you harvest chickweed. Clip the tender tips only and you will save yourself immense work. (If you inadvertently harvest some stringy stems, save them for making salve.) In New Zealand, chickweed can be found blossoming even on winter days. Seeds are also edible, though tedious to collect in quantity.

FOOD USE: Nibble chickweed tips. Add to salads, stir-fries, and curries. Steam as a potherb and drizzle with herb butter or herbal vinaigrette. Mix into pesto, or blend with chickpeas for a green hummus. Make chickweed fritters, or chickweed and halibut burgers. Try a chickweed egg scramble or chickweed deviled eggs. Blend chickweed with apple juice and fresh mint for a chlorophyll-laden green drink.

HEALTH USE: Chickweed is low in calories and high in iron, phosphorus, calcium, magnesium, zinc, potassium, and vitamins A and C. Add chickweed to ointments and poultices to relieve itching of insect bites and rashes. A student reported how she'd been accidentally splashed in her eye with essential oils. Her doctor's remedy provided no relief, and in desperation she turned to the chickweed growing prolifically outside her door. She did a series of chickweed poultices that dramatically eased her eye pain and inflammation. Herbalist Susun S. Weed also recommends chickweed poultices for eye diseases, including treating children's pink eye, and reminds users to apply fresh plant for each application. Additionally, Weed suggests chickweed tincture for "dissolving cysts and benign tumors." In clinical trials in vitro and in rodents, chickweed was demonstrated to have "antiviral, hepatoprotective, and antiobesity properties."

OTHER: *Stellaria* is well liked by domestic chickens, rabbits, and pigs. Feed seeds to caged birds. Chickweed seeds can remain viable for up to 6 decades. While some gardeners scorn chickweed's enthusiasm for growing, others use this to their advantage. Cornell University reports: "In the Rhine Valley of Germany, many of the vineyards are planted on extremely steep slopes. Farmers plant chickweed on the slope to hold soil in place, to conserve water and to help keep soil temperature constant. Scandinavian orchardists plant chickweed as a ground cover under the trees, believing that it brings better yields and higher quality fruit." In Australia, herbalist Robyn Kirby relies on chickweed in her canine formulas to relieve itching.

CLOVER
Trifolium species
Pea family (Fabaceae), Clover tribe (Trifolieae)

Clovers thrive in meadows and roadsides from Alaska to New Zealand. The clover blossom has 30 to 40 small flowers per cluster; colors vary with species from white to pink to reddish-purple. Leaves are typically 3 per stem. It's considered good luck to find a 4-leaf clover, but I think that we're all lucky to have the bountiful gifts every clover offers.

DERIVATION OF NAME: *Trifolium* refers to the typical "three leaves."

OTHER NAMES: white clover (*Trifolium repens*), red clover (*T. pratense*), Alsike clover (*T. hybridum*).

RANGE: Most areas of Alaska except north of the Brooks Range.

HARVESTING DIRECTIONS: Pick leaves and blossoms at their prime; harvest flowers before they start to turn brown.

FOOD USE: Infuse fresh or dried flowers as a beverage tea; experience the taste difference between traditional hot-water infused teas and steeping overnight in cold water. Process your favorite clover tea into a floral jelly. Dry and grind clover blossoms and use this gluten-free flour in baking. Bake a batch of wild berry and clover cookies. Add leaves and flowers to your wild greens blends for soups and stir-fries. Serve your family a Clover Blossom Spoonbread (ledameredith.com/clover-blossom-spoonbread-recipe). Experience a luscious white clover pudding (gathervictoria.com/2015/06/09/white-clover-pudding-a-recipe-for-comfort-healing).

HEALTH USE: Herbalist Rosemary Gladstar combines red clover flowers, violet leaves and flowers, and calendula flowers as a syrup for lymphatic congestion (Alaskans could substitute bedstraw for the calendula). She also advocates a "vitamin tonic" tea that includes clover, nettle, mint, and violet. Red clover blossoms, in particular, have been used by herbalists to support liver function and as a phytogestrogenic support for women undergoing menopause. A 12-week placebo-controlled randomized study of healthy menopausal women found that a daily supplement of red clover extract had positive effect on bone health. All women in the red clover group had improvements in bone mass density.

OTHER: Prior to World War II, white clover seed was a standard ingredient in pasture and lawn seed mixes. Besides attracting honeybees, clover "provides several environmental services such as N [nitrogen] fixation and protection against soil erosions," according to feedipedia.org. "Because of these characteristics, white clover is of particular interest in organic farming systems." Clover is highly drought tolerant, and is a high-protein source in pasture, hay, and silage for livestock. Danish researchers are exploring use of clover as a plant-based protein source and soy alternative.

CAUTION: Clover can cause digestive upset and bloating if eaten in excess. Clover's digestibility is said to be improved by presoaking leaves and flowers in saltwater for several hours or overnight.

HORSETAIL
Equisetum species
Horsetail family (Equisetaceae)

Horsetail is considered to be a living fossil, a remnant from dinosaur days, when it grew to over 90 feet high. Today's horsetails tend to be a mere 1 to 2 feet tall. Field horsetail, *Equisetum arvense*, is a widespread Alaskan species and the predominant one for health purposes. It has 2 growth forms, the early brown stalk with a swollen, cone-like head that releases clouds of spores, and a later green vegetative sterile stalk, whose branches lengthen with age. The woodland horsetail *E. silvaticum* has branches that are softer to the touch and more feathery in appearance and bear sporeheads atop the green stems. (See *Flora of Alaska* by Eric Hultén for a full range of species.)

DERIVATION OF NAME: *Equisetum* translates as "field horse bristle."

OTHER NAMES: puzzlegrass, scouring rush, field horsetail (*Equisetum arvense*), wood horsetail (*E. silvaticum*).

RANGE: Throughout Alaska.

HARVESTING DIRECTIONS: Pick the green stalks in spring, while the branches are still pointing upwards. Older plants may be used as poultice or for pot-scrubbing.

FOOD USE: Horsetail is used primarily as a mineral-rich tea. Its texture deters use as a potherb; however, I have added finely chopped young vegetative growth to wilderness spring soups to extend supplies. Tuberous root growths of field horsetail, collected just after snowmelt, are a popular food among various Alaskan indigenous people. Inuit typically gather them from the caches of mice or voles and eat them raw with seal oil.

HEALTH USE: Alutiiq and Athabascan people apply mashed vegetative stem as poultices for skin troubles, including pimples, cuts, and scrapes. (Ashes from burned plants are also used.) Nelson Island Yup'ik use infusions and decoctions of vegetative portion of field and wood horsetails for internal bleeding. I successfully used horsetail poultices to eliminate a highly painful cyst. Iranian and Turkish clinical trials compared horsetail ointment with zinc oxide and concluded "equisetum extract ointment produced the best wound healing." *Equisetum* was also trialed on women with episiotomy wounds (surgical cuts to the vagina during childbirth) and found that it facilitates healing and pain reduction. German Commission E (a scientific advisory board) approves use of field horsetail tea as a diuretic for post-traumatic edema, urinary tract infections, and inflammations. South American trials further substantiated horsetail's diuretic properties. Herbalist David Hoffman, President of the American Herbalists Guild, notes horsetail's "toning and astringent actions make it invaluable in the treatment of incontinence and bed wetting in children. It is considered a specific in cases of inflammation or benign enlargement of the prostate gland."

OTHER: When camping, scrub pots with mature horsetail. Condition your hair with horsetail teas. If your plants are troubled by aphids, fill a quart spray bottle with horsetail (or horsetail-nettle tea) and 5 drops eco-friendly dish soap and spritz your plants.

CAUTION: Internally, use only young field horsetail plants, and consume in moderation. Old plants can irritate the kidneys. Raw horsetails contain thiaminase, a vitamin B–depleting enzyme. Animals that overgraze horsetail can suffer convulsions and loss of muscular control. Vitamin B1 shots are used as an antidote. (Thiaminase is deactivated by heat.)

LAMB'S QUARTER

Chenopodium album
Amaranth family (Amaranthaceae),
Goosefoot subfamily (Chenopodiaceae)

When my friend Ellie had a subscription market garden in Palmer, Alaska, the first of her spring deliveries always included a generous bag of lamb's quarter. Later in the season, when she supplied the "usual" vegetables, folks would beg her for more of that tasty spring green, few realizing it was a garden "weed" they had been eating. Do get to know this generous garden volunteer! Lamb's quarter is another of the globetrotters, ranging from northern Alaska to southern New Zealand. Stems average 1 to 3 feet but can grow even taller in compost with animal manures. Flowers are inconspicuous and are followed by abundant seed that self-sows.

DERIVATION OF NAME: *Chenopodium* translates as "goosefoot," referring to the shape of the leaf; *album* means "white" and indicates the whitish water-repellant bloom on the leaf.

OTHER NAMES: fat hen, pigweed.

RANGE: Southeast Alaska to Kodiak and the western Yukon, and north to the Brooks Range.

HARVESTING DIRECTIONS: Clip the aboveground portion in spring before flowering. The newest leaf growth can be gathered into summer. Collect seeds late summer to early autumn.

FOOD USE: Fill a breakfast wrap with sautéed lamb's quarter and bell peppers, scrambled eggs, and seasonings. Sauté with onions, garlic, and salmon for a pita bread filler, or add some beans to this filling to top a taco. Make a Greek salad with young lamb's quarter, cherry tomatoes, feta cheese, thin-sliced red onion, and kalamata olives. Steam lamb's quarter with quinoa and toss with your wild green pesto for a cool salad. For year-round use, blanch 1 minute, cool, drain, and package in freezer bags or containers. Use lamb's quarter seeds (related to quinoa*) in winter soups and stews, or as a substitute for poppy seeds in cakes and breads.

HEALTH USE: Greens are high in protein (4.2%), essential fatty acids, vitamins A, B and C, and the minerals iron, calcium, phosphorus, and potassium. A clinical review from India notes that the common lamb's quarter, *C. album*, improves appetite, acts as a nourishing body tonic, is antiparasitic, and relieves abdominal pain. And, in Ayurvedic medicine, it is used to treat cough and nervous afflictions. Externally, lamb's quarter is used by Athabascans as a poultice for wounds and inflammation.

OTHER: An Indian study by Poonia and Upadhayay states: "Interest in *C. album* as a valuable food source has renewed in Asia in recent years because of its versatility and its ability to grow under stressed conditions like low rainfall, high altitude, thin cold air, hot sun, and sub-freezing temperature. Increased awareness in the society and consequently more use of this plant may go a long way towards preventing not only deficiency diseases and age-related muscular degeneration-related disorders, but also protect against chronic degenerative diseases, such as cancer and cardiovascular disorders which ultimately will be highly beneficial to the rural community."

CAUTION: Lamb's quarter contains oxalic acid (as does spinach and most garden greens). Oxalic acid is reduced by cooking. See dock and sorrel on page 162 for more details.

*Quinoa, popular with vegetarians and those on gluten-free diets, is seed harvested from the lamb's quarter cousin *Chenopodium quinoa*. Lamb's quarter seed is smaller than the commercial variety, but can be used similarly by avid foragers.

NETTLE
Urtica gracilis, U. lyallii
Nettle family (Urticaceae)

EDIBLE STAGE | FLOWER STAGE

I tend to love the "wild things" that others love to hate, and nettles are no exception. I've planted a "living wall" of nettles surrounding my home garden to deter my grazing horses from leaning into my vegetable patch. Its proximity to my kitchen encourages me to harvest new nettle growth regularly, which significantly extends the forage season. Nettles are incredibly easy to identify. Look closely and you'll notice the soft but stinging hairs (trichomes) on both leaf and stem. Leaves are arranged in pairs that rotate along the stem; individual leaves have serrated edges. Early spring plants are often tinged with red. Later in the season, small flowers grow in drooping clusters at the intersection of leaves and stem. Lightly brush a plant and you'll immediately know why it's called "stinging nettle."

DERIVATION OF NAME: *Urtica* is from the Latin root *uro*, "to burn."

OTHER NAMES: stinging nettle, burning nettle, itchweed, *paumnaq* (Yup'ik), *t'óok'* (Tlingit).

RANGE: Southeast Alaska to the Interior.

HARVESTING DIRECTIONS: To avoid stinging, wear long-sleeved clothes and gloves as you harvest. Pick plants when under 1 foot in height. Avoid consuming older leaves and flowering plants, as they can irritate the kidneys. For year-round use, freeze or dry spring nettles. Harvest seeds when ripe. Dig roots in the fall or early spring.

FOOD USE: Nesto (nettle pesto) is a perennial favorite and freezes well. (Substitute steamed drained nettles for basil.) Use thick nesto as a spread on garlic bread or as a pizza base, or thin nesto with extra oil for a vinaigrette. Combine young nettle leaves with potatoes and salmon in a chowder. Try a nettle walnut sauce on halibut. Simmer nettles lightly as a potherb; save the cooking water as tonic tea or soup stock. Add powdered dry nettles to smoothies and seasoning blends. Add nettle seeds to trail bars and fruit-nut balls.

HEALTH USE: Nettle leaves contain an alphabet of vitamins and minerals, from A to Zinc. They are a rich store of essential amino acids, comparable to beans and chicken, and nettle-leaf flour is higher in protein than wheat or barley. Iron-rich nettles are an excellent tea for anemics, and menstruating and lactating women. Numbers of studies demonstrate ability of nettle leaves to lower high blood pressure, alleviate rheumatic pain, and enhance immune response. *The Journal of Herbal Pharmacotherapy* published a 6-month double-blind placebo-controlled clinical trial using *Urtica* root in the treatment of benign prostatic hyperplasia; 81% of those in the *Urtica* group showed improved lower urinary tract symptoms compared to 16% in the placebo group. Positive effects were maintained over at least 18 months, and no major side effects occurred.

OTHER: Nettles offer countless opportunities for a hungry and stressed planet. Researcher Tigist Tadesse Shonte attributes its limited use as a food source to "seasonality, the fear of the stinging hairs, lack of commercial availability and the stigma related to stinging nettles being associated with famine/poor man's food." Besides food, nettle yields strong fibers, traditionally woven by indigenous people as nets, string, and ropes. Fashion houses in Germany, Austria, and Italy now have nettle-fabric product lines in production. More nettles are needed by the growing industries. Unlike cotton with its cocktail of chemicals, nettles can be grown pesticide free. Nettles offer commercial opportunities for green-minded entrepreneurs, while providing quality habitat for butterflies and songbirds.

CAUTION: Don't eat nettles raw. Cooking or drying nettles deactivates the sting. Nettle rash can be treated with mashed dock, plantain, jewelweed, fiddlehead chaff, or nettle juice itself.

PINEAPPLE WEED

Matricaria discoidea, aka *Matricaria matricariodes*
Aster family (Asteraceae), Aster subfamily,
Chamomile tribe (Anthemideae)

This ground-hugging wild chamomile thrives in sunny paths and waste areas. Rub the greenish-yellow flowerhead between your hands and notice the fresh pineapple scent. Leaves are feathery, finely dissected, on stems 3 to 12 inches high. The plants, which frequent hard-packed soil, may be erect or sprawling.

DERIVATION OF NAME: Pineapple weed's botanical name *Matricaria* translates as "dear mother" and refers to its historical use by mothers and their newborns; *discoidea* means "without rays," which describes how the flowers lack the ray petals typical of other chamomile species.

OTHER NAMES: wild chamomile, Alaskan chamomile, dog fennel.

RANGE: Most of Alaska, though rarely in the northernmost Arctic.

HARVESTING DIRECTIONS: Pick the flowers at their peak in mid-summer. Gather foliage throughout the growing season.

FOOD USE: For a cool beverage with delightful aroma and taste, steep 4 tablespoons fresh chopped pineapple weed flowers in a quart of cold water overnight. For kids, blend this cold tea half and half with apple or pineapple juice and freeze as popsicles. Garnish salads with wild chamomile flowers. Add greens and flowers to pestos. Infuse pineapple weed flowers in butter as a spread for pineapple weed flower muffins. Blend chopped flowers with coconut yogurt for a dairy-free treat. For winter, try mulled wild chamomile; blend dry flowers with a pinch of cinnamon, cloves, and nutmeg, and steep in boiled water for 20 minutes.

HEALTH USE: In Aleut culture, wild chamomile flower-leaf teas are a general tonic for ailments ranging from colic to constipation. Yup'ik Natives drink tea for colds. Athabascan, Dena'ina, and Alutiiq mothers drink the tea after childbirth and give drops of it to newborns. Rub the tea on the gums of teething infants. Wild chamomile is a gentle calmer for relieving family or school stress. Gayla Pederson of Kodiak reports how her fisherman partner was regularly experiencing extreme night terrors; he began a nightly regime of a full dropper of chamomile glycerite* 30 minutes before bed. "By the end of that month the nightmares had subsided almost completely and now happened only once every 3 to 6 months and usually under times of extreme stress like getting ready for fishing season," she reported. A microbiological research article documents antimicrobial effects of various *Matricaria* species and lists diverse uses of wild chamomile including gastrointestinal system disorders (flatulence, stomachache), throat inflammations, wounds, and ulcers.

OTHER: Rub pineapple weed flowers between your hands to remove odors from handling fish, garlic, or cleaning products. Place fresh or dried wild chamomile in a mesh bag and add to your evening bath to promote relaxation.

CAUTION: Some individuals are sensitive to handling or ingesting chamomile.

*A glycerite is made by steeping an herb in 60% vegetable glycerin/40% water solution for 3 weeks, and then straining. Vegetable glycerin is superb with aromatic herbs like chamomiles, mints, etc.

PLANTAIN

Plantago major (common plantain), *P. macrocarpa* (Alaska plantain)
Plantain family (Plantaginaceae), Plantain tribe (Plantagineae)

Common plantain has broad leaves with 5 to 9 conspicuous veins. Leaves are in a basal arrangement that often lie close to the ground as though stepped on. The inconspicuous flowers grow on leafless stalks; most evident are the yellow stamens that hang from the stem and "hula" in the wind. Alaska plantain bears narrower and much longer leaves than common plantain. (See goosetongue on page 50 for comparison.)

DERIVATION OF NAME: *Plantago* means "sole of the foot." "White man's footstep" is a common name for common plantain as its migration pattern mirrored the footsteps of European traders and settlers.

OTHER NAMES: cart-track plant, soldier's herb, waybread.

RANGE: Common plantain frequents roadsides and waste places from Southeast Alaska to the Brooks Range. Alaska plantain grows in wet places and beaches from Southeast to south coastal Alaska and in the Aleutian Islands.

HARVESTING DIRECTIONS: For food use, pick small tender leaves of common plantain in spring. Alaska plantain has a much longer season for harvesting edible greens. Collect seeds in late summer by rubbing the mature stalk between the hands and blowing lightly to remove the chaff.

FOOD USE: Use tender leaves in spring rolls, veggie dishes, scrambled eggs, and stews. Tougher leaves can be pureed in cream soups and green drinks. Try blending plantain with nut milk, honey, your favorite wild berries, a sprig of mint, and a dash of honey. Rub leaves with olive oil and nutritional yeast and seasonings and dehydrate as a snack chip. Toast seeds in a skillet; they have a flavor reminiscent of artichokes. Add seeds to muffins in place of poppy seeds.

HEALTH USE: Herbalists use common plantain as an expectorant, anti-inflammatory, and pain-relieving herb for respiratory issues; it is used in syrups, teas, and tinctures. A Bulgarian clinical trial using a *P. major* preparation on patients with chronic bronchitis confirmed improvements in 80% of those treated. Another report by Norwegian researcher Anne Berit Samuelsen notes: "A range of biological activities has been found from [*Plantago major*] plant extracts including wound healing activity, anti-inflammatory, analgesic, antioxidant, weak antibiotic, immuno-modulating and antiulcerogenic activity." Alaskan Aleut infuse Alaska plantain root as a tonic tea. Alutiiq apply common plantain leaves as a poultice for cracked feet. I've personally witnessed the power of plantain poultices in treating infected wilderness wounds, even reversing the red streaks of spreading infection. Plantain ointments and tinctures are an essential in my travel first-aid kit. Seeds, which are related to psyllium, are a natural laxative. Add 1 tablespoon ground seed in a glass of water, stir, and drink. Make certain to stay well hydrated.

OTHER: Plantain botanical extracts are used to reduce skin reddening. Phytessence™ Plantago is one product clinically shown "to reduce the healing time of UV damaged skin by almost 50%." Use plantain in your skin lotions and herbal baths for skin rashes. Use powdered plantain leaves as foot powder. Leaves were traditionally placed in shoes to prevent blisters.

CAUTION: Some individuals experience allergic reactions to plantain. The seeds should not be taken as a bulk laxative by those with GI obstructions.

PUFFBALL

Lycoperdon perlatum (common puffball),
Calvatia borealis (boreal puffball)
Agaricaceae family

Puffballs get their common name from their habit of "puffing" dust-like clouds of spores from their mature fruitbodies when stepped on or disturbed. Unlike fungi that have spores carried on their gills, puffballs spores mature internally. They are a distinctive fungus, round to pear-shaped in appearance. Size varies from marble to baseball and larger. *Lycoperdon* and *Calvatia* species share the same genus and use.

DERIVATION OF NAME: *Lycoperdon* translates as "wolf's fart." *Calvatia* means "bald head."

OTHER NAME: devil's snuffbox.

RANGE: Throughout Alaska.

HARVESTING DIRECTIONS: Cut each puffball in half and examine carefully. Discard any that reveal the outline of a mushroom cap and stem inside, as this could be the button stage of the deadly *Amanita*. Specimens suitable for consumption are creamy white and homogeneous inside; flesh should look like smooth cream cheese (see center of photo). Avoid eating any with yellow, discolored, or mushy flesh, or with black or jelly-like insides (see top of photo).

FOOD USE: Peel large puffballs before cooking for best results. Dice puffballs and scramble with eggs. Add puffball cubes to pasta sauces or miso soup. Dip large puffball slices in egg, coat with flour, spices, and nutritional yeast or parmesan, and sauté in oil until brown. Marinade puffballs with sweet and sour sauce and sesame seeds and add to stir-fries.

HEALTH USE: A Turkish clinical trial published in *Cytotechnology* noted that many fungi have antibiotic, antiviral, and anticancer effects. The researchers stated that an extract of the giant puffball *Calvatia gigantea* "may be a significant agent for treatment of lung cancer as a single agent or in combination with other drugs."

OTHER: Puffballs thrive in lawns and in hard-packed gravel of abandoned roads. Though stepping on old puffballs and watching them spout spores is a favorite activity for kids and the playful-at-heart, the practice should be discouraged as inhaling fungal spores can irritate bronchial linings and allergies. Wild Food UK states that a single raindrop hitting a mature common puffball can release over a million spores and that inhaled in large quantities can cause inflammation of the alveoli in the lungs. Those interested in foraging additional mushroom species are advised to see Gary A. Laursen and Neil McArthur's *Alaska's Mushrooms*.

WORMWOOD

Artemisia tilesii
Aster family (Asteraceae), Aster subfamily,
Chamomile tribe (Anthemideae)

LEAF IN SPRING   FLOWER STAGE

According to Robert Fortuine's *Alaska Medicine*, "no single plant has had a wider range of medicinal uses in Alaska than *Artemisia tilesii*." This plant ranges from the Arctic to the Aleutians and Southcentral Alaska (being noticeably absent in Southeast). The irregular lobed leaves are silvery underneath. Crush a leaf and you'll notice a distinctive aroma. Flowers are nondescript balls, yellow-green to brown in color. Stems generally grow 1 to 3 feet in height, with exceptional specimens reaching 6 feet.

DERIVATION OF NAME: *Artemisia* honors Artemis, Greek goddess of the moon and female energies.

OTHER NAMES: stinkweed, caribou leaves, Alaskan sage, *caiggluut* (Yup'ik); *ts'elbeni* (Dena'ina), *caik* (Alutiiq), *Sudigak* (Athabascan).

RANGE: Northern Panhandle to the Bering Sea and Arctic Ocean.

HARVESTING DIRECTIONS: Favorite harvest times and methods vary regionally throughout Alaska from early spring leaves, to summer tops (containing leaves and flowers), to brown wintered-over leaves. Experiment freely to determine which you prefer.

FOOD USE: Wormwood is quite bitter, and food use is only as a spice. A pinch, added to goose, duck, or salmon (or in villages, seal and whale) enhances digestibility of high-fat animal foods. Take a cooking tip from Japanese chefs, who typically combine bitter with sour to create a savory umami flavor. Chef Vikram Khatri states: "Bitter takes the dish to the next level, but it has to be cooked in a palatable way without letting the bitterness overpower the palate."

HEALTH USE: When I traveled throughout Alaska years ago and interviewed village locals, wormwood was the plant shown to me time and time again. Using wormwood as tea for colds and flu is a cross-cultural application, as are poultices of the crushed fresh or dried plant for wounds. Apply wormwood hot packs for sore muscles and joint pain. Do a steam inhalation for respiratory congestion. Dip wormwood in hot water and briskly switch yourself in a sauna to promote sweating and healing; you'll notice your breath begin to smell like wormwood. A Nome woman reported how wormwood poultices healed skin sores that had defied 2 years of pharmaceutical treatments. Ever since I added wormwood tincture to my air travel kit (taking a dropperful before, during, and after transcontinental air journeys), I've been free of the "post-flight bronchitis bouts" that used to plague me. In my household, anyone who sneezes, sniffles, or has the slightest scratchy throat is invited to a dose of wormwood. Campers can chew roots for sore-throat medicine.

OTHER: Add wormwood to sore muscle liniments and massage oils, as well as salves for eczema and other skin ailments. Some Alaskan fishermen bathe hands in wormwood tea or liniment before and after handling fish to prevent fish handler's disease (small cuts that get infected). Besides physical healing, wormwood is also traditionally used for spiritual cleansing and protection. In Southwest Alaska, Yup'ik rub wormwood over a person's body for purification following illness or death of a family member. Dried wormwood is also burned as incense to clean sickrooms or spaces where there has been emotional upset.

CAUTION: Use wormwood internally in small quantities only. Check with your doctor if pregnant or on medications.

YARROW

Achillea borealis

Aster family (Asteraceae), Aster subfamily, Chamomile tribe

Yarrow is a plant that changed my life. While living at my remote cabin, and sawing wood, I sliced my thumb to the bone. With pressure failing to slow the bleeding, I began to panic. Medical help was a 7-mile walk and 20-mile drive away. Achilles, I remembered reading, had staunched his soldier's wounds with yarrow. Could this weed actually help? I tentatively chewed yarrow leaves and applied to my thumb. The bleeding abruptly stopped, the wound healed speedily, and my interest in the power of herbs to heal was permanently ignited. Yarrow's French name, *millefoil*, means "thousand leaf," aptly describing the appearance of the leaves. (In Alutiiq, it's *Qangananguaq*, meaning "squirrel's tail.") Yarrow is a common perennial plant, with stems to 2 feet high and a flat-topped cluster of white flowers (with both petals and disk flowers). Leaves and flowers are aromatic.

DERIVATION OF NAME: *Achillea* is named after Achilles, whose mother dipped him in a yarrow bath to make him invincible; she held him by the heel, thus his vulnerable "Achilles heel." *Borealis* refers to "boreal" (the northern regions).

OTHER NAMES: northern yarrow, nosebleed, soldier's woundwort, poor man's pepper, staunchwort, sneezeweed, field hop, *xil sgun.ulaa* (Haida, "fragrant leaves/medicine").

RANGE: Throughout Alaska except for the extreme north Arctic.

HARVESTING DIRECTIONS: Collect spring leaves. Harvest flowering tops in summer. Dig roots fall or early spring.

FOOD USE: Yarrow can easily overwhelm food with bitterness, unless you take time to learn its secrets. Leaves must be extremely young. Use a light touch, and add at the very end of the cooking period. Alan Bergo's *Forager Chef* blog recipes include an aromatic oil blending ½ cup blanched parsley with ¼ cup yarrow. He recommends yarrow minced with red pepper added to a garlicky penne pasta. Add finely chopped young leaves to your omelet. Steam mussels or clams, skewer onto yarrow stems, and smoke over a campfire or barbecue.

HEALTH USE: Yarrow's use spans cultures and centuries. Teas (flowering herb) are traditional for colds and flu and to reduce fever. Crushed leaves staunch wounds and nosebleeds. Aleuts drank yarrow teas for tuberculosis, Alutiiq for coughs and congestion, and Athabascans for kidney troubles. Tlingit used leaf poultices for menstrual cramps and rheumatic pain. Measles, inflammation, and internal bleeding were all treated with yarrow. Yarrow's been described as one of the most widely used medicinal plants on the planet; the entire herb inhibits microbes and also has an astringent action, tightening and toning injured tissue. Inhale a yarrow herbal steam for stuffy sinuses. Chew a root to numb a wilderness toothache. I routinely use yarrow root tincture as topical application for dental hygiene treatments.

OTHER: At an herbal conference years ago, I sampled an excellent yarrow beer; moderation is essential as yarrow brew is reputed highly intoxicating. According to Daniel Moerman and Wendy Applequist in *Economic Botany*, animal clinical trials have "shown that yarrow is generally safe and well tolerated." They believe that the typical warning not to use yarrow during pregnancy "is based on a single low-quality rat study the results of which were incorrectly interpreted."

CAUTION: Some individuals are allergic to yarrow. Consult your physician if on blood-thinners or medications.

Forests & Open Woods

Woodlands are a realm of vast opportunities for foragers. Thirty-five percent of Alaska is covered by forests. Southeast Alaska's 19 million acres (making up 5% of Alaska) is most densely forested; primary species of the Tongass and south coastal Alaska are Sitka spruce, western hemlock, and western and yellow cedar.

The Boreal forest extends from the Kenai Peninsula to the Brooks Range foothills and includes balsam poplar, aspen, birch, larch, and spruce. Forest soils are often acidic and hospitable to many understory plants prized by foragers, including berries and fiddlehead ferns.

SPRUCE
Picea species
Pine family (Pinaceae)

My favorite class "opener" for kids, adults, or Elderhostel is to share the creation tale of the Dena'ina people. As I remember from listening to elder Peter Kalifornsky decades ago: *The Creator of the earth made a partner for every single plant so that one could be a helper to the other. The only plant that had no partner was spruce, because spruce was to be the helpmate for humankind. Every single part of spruce has a use.* I would then pass around twigs, spruce tips, bark, spruce sap, a slab of wood, and spruce root (written on slips of paper or the "real" thing), and students would brainstorm how spruce could possibly have been used. See Priscilla Russell Kari's *Tanaina Plantlore* for an exhaustive list of Native applications to stimulate your own deep relations with spruce. Both black and white spruce have 4-sided needles that roll easily between the fingertips; black spruce has dense orange fuzz on its new growth stems, whereas white has hairless twigs. Sitka spruce has needles that are flattened and resist rolling. All spruce are user friendly to foragers.

DERIVATION OF NAME: *Picea* is the classical Latin name for spruce.

OTHER NAMES: white spruce (*P. glauca*), Sitka spruce (*P. sitchensis*), black spruce (*P. mariana*), Lutz spruce (hybrid).

RANGE: Southeast Alaska to the Brooks Range.

HARVESTING DIRECTIONS: Gather spruce tips when newly emerged (the bright green spring growth at the end of spruce branches). Gather inner bark from branch cuttings in early spring when the sap is flowing.

FOOD USE: In a Cordova, Alaska, class years ago, student Meadow Bejarano whipped up a spruce tip salsa that has been a regular ever since. Steep overnight 1 to 2 cups young chopped spruce tips blended with diced tomatoes, tomato paste, garlic, lemon and lime juice, diced onion, and bell pepper, and seasonings and tabasco as desired. It's fantastic as a dip with corn chips or a topping on tacos. Spruce tip tea was a stable drink in my bush cabin life. In winter, I would pour boiling water on the dried spruce tips. Sometimes I'd add rose hips, cinnamon sticks, cloves, and honey. Spring was "cool-aid" time: I'd steep chopped fresh tips overnight in cold water for maximum vitamin C and flavor. Inner bark is a traditional survival food, eaten raw or boiled, or dried and ground into flour.

HEALTH USE: Some foragers simmer the spruce tips in boiled water, which extracts many tannins, making it quite useful as an antiseptic wash. (The latter was highly useful as a nasal wash when I suffered a sinus infection after exposure to mold.) Captain Cook rationed spruce beer to his crew, keeping spirits up and bodies free of scurvy. Spruce jelly and syrup soothe sore throats. Spruce sap and melted pitch serve as medicinal plasters to protect wounds from infection. A graphically illustrated Finnish clinical trial using refined *Picea* resin to treat chronic wounds concluded "it is indisputable that the establishment of the efficacy of spruce resin in the treatment of chronic wounds fulfils the criterion of a new innovation of an old folkloristic medical therapy."

OTHER: Grind inner bark for a foot powder. Koyukon Athabascans believe white spruce has a potent and kindly spirit.

CAUTION: Excess decoctions (simmered tea) can be irritating to the kidneys. Some individuals are allergic to topically applied spruce resin.

BIRCH
Betula species
Birch family (Betulaceae)

Birches are dubbed "ladies of the forest" due to their elegant appearance. They range worldwide throughout the temperate regions. Alaska's commonly recognised white or gray-barked forest birches include paper birch (*B. papyrifera*), Kenai birch (*B. kenaica*), and Alaska birch (*B. neoalaskana*). Less well known are the "bonzais" of the birch world, the dwarf and shrub birches: *B. nana* and *B. glandulosa* of tundra, bogs, and swamps. Flowers of all species have drooping catkins, and stems have a distinctive sandpaper texture.

DERIVATION OF NAME: Birch is associated with the Sanskrit word *bhurja*, a tree whose bark is used for writing.

OTHER NAMES: lady birch, lady of the forest, paper birch, Kenai birch.

RANGE: Tree birches range from Kodiak, Kenai, and the Alaska Peninsula north to the Brooks Range, and lower Seward Peninsula; Southeast Alaska is the only region where both tree and shrubby birches are noticeably rare (occasionally cultivated).

HARVESTING DIRECTIONS: Collect sap of tree birches as winter ends when nights are still frosty and days above freezing (usually early April). Drill a ½-inch-diameter hole (at a slight upward angle) on the sunny side of the tree. Insert a sap tap (purchased or homemade) and hang a 5-gallon bucket to collect the sap. Cover with cheesecloth to keep out insects. Tapping is usually done over 3 weeks. Plug the hole with sphagnum moss when done. Collect spring birch leaves (from any species) for food purposes when bright green and the size of a mouse's ear. For health purposes, summer leaves and inner bark from a pruned branch (not the trunk) are used.

FOOD USE: Fresh, undiluted sap is a refreshing and nutritive tonic brew, akin to the taste of coconut water. It freezes well for winter use. It can also be flavored with berries or citrus as desired. Sap can be reduced at a 10-to-1 ratio for brewing vinegar or beer. Condensing sap to "birch syrup" is labor intensive. It takes an average of 100 gallons of sap to produce 1 gallon of syrup. For a DIY preparation, slowly evaporate the sap in a well-ventilated area until a dark, sweet syrup results. For personal inspiration for using birch syrup or to buy readymade birch products, see the Alaska Wild Harvest website (alaskabirchsyrup.com). Baby birch leaves, picked from any species soon after emergence, are a vitamin C-rich green. I've often added them to wilderness salads, soups, and stir-fries. Cambium from various tree species is a traditional subsistence food I always associate with famines, but the practicalselfreliance.com blog demos using dry ground cambium as a replacement for ¼ of the flour in shortbread cookies for a "buckwheat-like flavor."

HEALTH USE: Buds and leaves are antifungal; add to ointments for toe fungus or ringworm. Bark decoctions are a traditional wash for skin rashes and scratches and an ingredient in ointments for sore muscles and rheumatic pains. For birch leaf tea, 1 to 2 teaspoons of leaf is steeped in boiled water, then strained. An Iraqi clinical trial published in the *Journal of Pharmaceutical Biology* on birch leaf tea showed that "it exerted many pharmacological effects including anticancer, immunological, antiviral, antibacterial, antifungal, antiprotozoal, anti-inflammatory, and analgesic effects."

OTHER: During a sauna, switch yourself with a leafy birch branch to stimulate your skin.

CAUTION: The Iraqi trial mentioned above advises that birch leaf tea "should not be used for edema when there is reduced cardiac or kidney function." It recommends ensuring an ample fluid intake (minimum 2 litres) while taking birch. "No health hazards or side effects are known in conjunction with the proper administration of designated therapeutic dosages of birch leaves." It adds: "A fresh cup of tea is taken between meals 3 to 4 times a day." Contact dermatitis with birch outer bark is known to occur. Some individuals are sensitive to birch pollen and potentially to the salicylates in birch.

COTTONWOOD

Populus balsamifera, * *Populus tremuloides* (trembling /quaking aspen)
Willow family (Salicaceae)

BUDDING STAGE
(*P. balsamifera*)

COTTONWOOD LEAVES

In spring, cottonwood can be identified by scent alone. As its thick resinous buds open, the "smell of Alaska" perfumes the air. Follow your nose to the trees dressed in thick, gray-brown bark, deeply furrowed with age. Leaves are smooth, dark green above and paler underneath; in fall they turn a glorious gold. Trembling aspen is a tree 18 to 36 feet high with finely saw-toothed leaves borne on flattish stems; leaves "tremble" or "quake" in a breeze. Bark commonly has a yellow-green cast.

*Some botanists are lumpers and others splitters. Some consider *P. balsamifera* a separate species from *P. trichocarpa* (western balsam poplar). Eric Hultén in *Flora of Alaska* considers *P. trichocarpa* a subspecies of *P. balsamifera*. For foragers, it matters not, so long as the cottonwood "has the resinous 'balm of Gilead' buds."

DERIVATION OF NAME: *Populus balsamifera* translates as "balsam-bearing poplar."

OTHER NAMES: balsam poplar, balm of Gilead (*P. balsamifera*), *tsiquq* (Yup'ik).

RANGE: Balsam poplar ranges from the northern Panhandle to the Arctic. Trembling aspens grow from the Northern Kenai and Matanuska Region to the upper Alaska Peninsula and north through the Interior and Brooks Range. Cottonwood is a distinctive tree of gravel bars, river valleys, and alluvial plains. Trembling aspen is common in interior forests.

HARVESTING DIRECTIONS: Harvest cottonwood's resinous buds for salve making from fall through spring breakup before leaves emerge. Selectively harvest from multiple trees, allowing abundant buds for the tree's life cycle. Pick catkins in spring. Harvest bark from pruned branches of both species (easiest when the spring sap is flowing).

FOOD USE: Though not my favorite food, the vitamin C-rich catkins (drooping flowers) can be nibbled when hiking. At my wilderness cabin, I roasted and ground the catkins and added to muffins to replace up to ¼ the flour in the recipe. Historically, spring cambium was also eaten, often during famines.

HEALTH USE: Cottonwood's resinous buds are antibacterial, antifungal, and analgesic. Steep buds in your oil of choice (almond, olive, etc) in the top of a double boiler; the strained oil, thickened with beeswax, yields an exquisite "balm of Gilead" salve with high efficacy on wounds, rashes, fungal issues, piles, and sore knees. Buds steeped in grain alcohol yield a tincture used internally for wet or dry coughs and to lessen the risk of secondary respiratory infections. For external use, combine cottonwood buds with inner bark of aspen or cottonwood; steep in grain alcohol for 3 weeks, then strain and apply as a liniment for muscle aches and sprains. Teas and tinctures made from *Populus* cambium contain salicin; though not as fast acting as aspirin to ease headache, the poplars are far gentler on the stomach. Canadian clinical trials on cottonwood bark extracts confirm the "high potential of *P. balsamifera* as a complementary treatment derived from CEI [Cree Indian] traditional medicine, which can help combat the devastating effects of obesity, often leading to type 2 diabetes."

OTHER: Steep buds in a pot of water on the back of your wood-fired stove as a winter room freshener. Collect thick cottonwood bark from a fallen tree; I love using this fantastic easy-to-carve wood for spoons and Alaskan "bear paw" salad scoops. Athabascans used bark for making sun goggles and fishing floats. Alutiiqs carved bark for toys, gaming pieces, plates, net floats, labrets, animal figurines, and maskettes. Cottonwood is a popular wood for smoking fish.

CAUTION: Like willow and birch, cottonwood contains salicin and salicortin. Check with your doctor before using internally if you are hypersensitive to aspirin.

JUNIPER

Juniperus communis (common mountain juniper),
J. horizontalis (creeping juniper)
Cypress family, aka cedar family (Cupressaceae)

Alaska's junipers are usually prostrate shrubs. They are evergreen, with leaves in whorls of 3. Fruits are green the first year and ripen blue to blackish in the second or third year. Leaves of common juniper vary from short and curved to straight and long-pointed; leaves of creeping juniper are scale-like. Junipers are common on dry slopes and places with sandy, rocky soils.

DERIVATION OF NAME: Its name comes from the Latin *junio* and *parere*, meaning "to produce youth," referring to its evergreen branches.

OTHER NAMES: prickly juniper, *Juniperus communis*, creeping cedar (*J. horizontalis*).

RANGE: Common mountain juniper ranges from the Panhandle to Matanuska Valley and in an arc to the Brooks Range; creeping juniper occurs in a narrow band from Anchorage eastward to Canada.

HARVESTING DIRECTIONS: Harvest fruits in fall when ripe.

FOOD USE: Juniper's flavors are a cross between citrus and spruce. Use to spice winter stews, and in marinades for fish or wild game. Try making a juniper highbush cranberry jam, or juniper and wild berry syrup for your sourdough hotcakes. Add juniper berries to fermented sauerkraut. Juniper is key to fermented Sremka, a Bosnian brew that has been described as "the tastiest beverage you never heard of." Some Sremka brewers add lemon to the juniper ferment; others use the berries solo.

HEALTH USE: Common mountain juniper is traditionally used by herbalists for healing urinary tract infections. For sinus infection, inhale the steam from a pot of simmering branches. Soak juniper in your bath to help ease joint pain. For Alaska's diverse indigenous people, juniper tea is cold and flu medicine; berries are chewed or brewed into tea. Branches are burned as smudge to cleanse sickrooms and ward off illness. Clinical trials confirm that juniper essential oils have a potent bactericidal effect against Gram-positive and Gram-negative bacterial species as well as yeasts, yeast-like fungi, and skin fungi (dermatophytes). The *Croatian Journal Acta Pharmaceutica* says, "The strongest fungicidal activity was recorded against *Candida* spp." A trial by Fernandez and Crock published in *Pharmacognosy Journal* concludes that the lack of toxicity of common juniper's berry extracts and their strong inhibitory bioactivity against bacteria and cervical and colorectal carcinoma cells "indicates their potential in the treatment and prevention of selected autoimmune inflammatory diseases and some cancers."

OTHER: Gin obtains its predominant flavor from juniper berries. Add juniper to homemade cleaning products for its aromatic and bactericidal properties.

CAUTION: Juniper is not recommended for pregnant women or young children. Medical herbalist Richard Whelan states that the typical warning regarding juniper use by those with kidney disease is based on high dose juniper essential oil experiments on rats. However, the berries do demand respect. "For anyone new to using juniper," Whelan advises, "start with juniper at a very moderate level, build up the dose gradually, and not to use it for too long."

DEVIL'S CLUB

Oplopanax horridus (formerly *Echinopanax horridum*)
Ginseng family (Araliaceae)

FRUIT STAGE

SHOOTS STAGE

Devil's club stirs strong emotions ranging from contempt to deep reverence. This fierce-looking plant is often despised by hikers but revered by herbalists for its ginseng-like properties. Sharp prickles are borne on woody stems, 5 to 10 feet in height, and exist on the undersides of the lobed dinner-plate-sized leaves. The clusters of small white flowers mature as scarlet-red fruits, which form a striking contrast to autumn's golden leaves. Devil's club's prickles are sharp. If you whack them, you can experience festering sores from prickles embedded in your skin. Yet it's possible to gently stroke them upwards with bare hands. I love gently wading through thick *Oplopanax* stands.

DERIVATION OF NAME: *Oplopanax horridus* translates to "fiercely armored panacea."

OTHER NAMES: Alaskan ginseng, *s'áxt'* (Tlingit), *ts'iiłanjaaw* (Haida).

RANGE: Devil's club ranges from Southeast and Southcentral Alaska to Kodiak and the Kenai Peninsula and north to Matanuska Valley.

HARVESTING DIRECTIONS: The leaf shoots are edible for about 10 days in early spring, when they first emerge from the spiny stalks and before the leaf spines harden. Carefully separate the emerging soft-spiny leaf shoots and remove 1 or 2 from each cluster; do not collect the entire leaf cluster. Harvest stem and roots early spring or fall (for health use); replant the top 6 to 8 inches of the prickly stem to ensure repeated harvest. Scrape stems of the prickly brown outer bark and discard; peel the green cambium layer and use fresh or dried.

FOOD USE: Young leaf shoots are delicious pickled with baby fireweed shoots and fiddleheads. Devil's club Macadamia nut pesto was a Cordova class favorite. For a potluck or special spring celebration, try devil's club shoot tempura (together with dandelion buds and twisted stalk shoots). Nibble shoots raw or add to egg-salmon scrambles or fermented sauerkraut.

HEALTH USE: As typical of many ginseng family members, devil's club has an adaptogenic (body-balancing) effect. At NM Herb Center in Albuquerque, run by Dr. Tieraona Low Dog, devil's club root was used in its pharmacy as an aid for lowering high blood sugar. A client's blood sugar levels declined from 280 mg/dL and stabilized at 120 over a 6-week period by taking 2 teaspoons devil's club tincture in hot water (plus blueberry leaf tea 3 times daily). Devil's club was also used to raise low blood sugar. In Wrangell, Tlingit simmer a dozen 1-foot-long unpeeled stems, gathered spring or fall, in a large pot of water (along with a handful of Labrador tea) until a deep-amber brew results. This sits overnight, then gets strained and refrigerated and drunk daily as a health tonic to enhance immunity and help prevent cancer. During a Palmer herb class, an acupuncturist recorded pulses of participants comparing effects of ingesting devil's club root versus stem decoctions. With stem cambium teas, weak pulses consistently became stronger, and those with excess conditions moderated. Stem teas, for me, result in a calm alertness. I find devil's club chai (made from stem cambium) a great way to start my day. Herbalists also use devil's club teas and tinctures for colds, respiratory infections, chronic fatigue, and for extending the remission phase of rheumatoid arthritis. *In vitro* clinical studies showed that extracts of devil's club inhibit tuberculosis. Devil's club roots can be pulverized and applied as poultices for wounds, bee stings, shingles, and even infections resulting from being pricked by a devil's club spine.

OTHER: Devil's club has a deep spiritual tradition in indigenous villages. It features in ceremonies as well as purification rituals before hunting. In my home is a treasured necklace of hand-carved devil's club root beads bequeathed by a Tlingit elder.

CAUTION: Diabetics taking devil's club are advised to monitor insulin levels consistently as *Oplopanax* can affect dosages for oral hypoglycemics or insulin. Some individuals have allergies to devil's club. A forager who brewed a devil's club beer reports that all who drank it became ill.

SERVICEBERRY

Amelanchier alnifolia (western serviceberry),
A. florida (Pacific serviceberry)
Rose family (formerly Heath, Ericaceae)

Serviceberries grew on the hillside behind my first Alaskan coastal residence and I've fond memories of savoring delectable serviceberry pies. Though *Amelanchier* species are wide ranging in the North Temperate zone, they are only regionally available to Alaskans and well worth cultivating (see Other below). Fruits are borne on a woody shrub to small tree. Flowers are showy, with 5 white petals and 5 sepals. The lower margin of the leaf is smooth, whereas the upper has teeth. The fruits, which botanically are called pomes, are blue-black with many seeds.

DERIVATION OF NAME: *Amelanchier* may be derived from the Occitan *Amelanchièr*, for a European species.

OTHER NAMES: Juneberry, saskatoon, *gaawáq* (Tlingit), *gaan xaw.ulaa* (Haida).

RANGE: Sporadically through Southeast Alaska, Southcentral, and the Interior in moist woods to open places.

HARVESTING DIRECTIONS: Pick fruits when plump and blue-black.

FOOD USE: Nibble berries while hiking. Top your morning muesli. Add to pancakes and pies, breads and muffins, and crêpes. Stew the fruits. Make a steamed pudding. Dry as a raisin substitute. Alaskan dog mushers and outdoor enthusiasts may wish to blend dry fruits with dried pounded meat and melted animal fat into pemmican (dubbed the ultimate survival food).

HEALTH USE: Due to more extensive serviceberry range in Canada and the Lower 48, most healing uses are recorded from outside Alaska. Serviceberry teas have been used as cold, flu, and fever remedies, wound disinfectants, etc. A dissertation by Jian Albert Zhang states that studies of serviceberry fruit and leaf teas and extracts "validate traditional knowledge of the antidiabetic effects of serviceberry."

OTHER: The American Indian Health and Diet Project reports: "Young serviceberry stems, branches, and wood have been used in basketry, furniture making, rope making, arrow making and harpoon making, tool making, and in the construction of popgun pistols." Fruits were an esteemed food for the hungry explorers on the Lewis And Clark Expedition. In the Alaskan railbelt area, commercial serviceberry production is being trialed. Grow your own serviceberries from seed or shrub cuttings or rooted suckers.

CAUTION: Grazing animals eating 2 pounds per day of serviceberry shrubs have died. *Amelanchier* species, according to a Canadian government agency, contain "a large quantity of prunasin, which has a hydrogen cyanide (HCN) potential exceeding the level required to cause poisoning in cattle. HCN occurs in the twigs before the leaves appear and during the bloom period. The level of HCN potential is highest in new-growth twigs, especially during dry years." Wilted leaves are also toxic. Serviceberry fruits and dry leaves, on the other hand, have been safely used by diverse cultures for millennia.

CURRANT
Ribes species
Gooseberry family (Grossulariaceae)

The gooseberry family has many representatives throughout Alaska, all forager friendly. Growth habits vary from trailing to upright (to 6 feet high); many thrive around old stumps. Depending on species, flowers may be upright or in drooping clusters (white, pinkish, or greenish in color). Individual flowers have 5 small petals and 5 stamens; sepals are united. The nicknames skunk currant and stink currant refer to the pungency of the lobed leaves of *Ribes glandulosum* and *R. bracteosum* (aka trailing northern black currant). The prized red currant (*R. triste*) has smooth bark that shreds easily, and smooth, red fruits. *R. lacustre* goes by names varying from bristly black currant to gooseberry to dog bramble.

DERIVATION OF NAME: *Ribes* is from the Arabic name for a plant with sour sap.

OTHER NAMES: *shaax* (Tlingit, *R. bracteosum*), *gaga giga*, brown bear's berry (Dena'ina, *R. hudsonianum*).

RANGE: Southeast Alaska to the northern Alaska Peninsula and northward to the Brooks Range.

HARVESTING DIRECTIONS: For preserves, gather fruits when plump but before fully ripe, which is when they are higher in pectin. For general food use, harvest at full maturity. Pick young leaves for tea. Harvest roots or stems fall or early spring.

FOOD USE: Currants are renowned as preserves (including currant-mint jelly for wild game). Currant muffins and cobblers are popular. Add currants to salsa, tacos, syrup, and trail bars, as well as liqueurs or mead (honey wine). Dry and powder the berries and add a teaspoon currant powder to fortify your morning smoothie or green drink. Combine fruits with fresh or fully dry leaves in beverage teas.

HEALTH USE: Currants are a superb source of vitamin C, yielding as high as 250 mg per 100 g of juice, even after 6 months of storage. Fruits contain both omega-3 and omega-6 essential fatty oils. Alaskan Alutiiq and Dena'ina use currants as a body-strengthening tonic for those with general ill health. Clinical *Ribes* trials substantiate the potent anti-inflammatory, antioxidant, and antimicrobial effects of currants on a myriad of disease states. They are said to protect and support digestive, circulatory, and nervous systems in particular. A Serbian study, published in *Medical Principles and Practice*, on the spasm-relieving effects of currants "shows that common gastrointestinal disorders could be treated by the functional food." A Japanese study by Nanashima and Horie further demonstrated that *Ribes* extract "has phytoestrogen activity in hair follicles and contributes to the alleviation of hair loss in a menopausal model in rats." Yakutat Tlingit as well as Eyak, Alutiiq, and Athabascan Natives have also used stem/bark decoctions for treating sore eyes.

OTHER: In the laboratory, the cultivated black currant *R. nigrum* is most often analyzed, but Alaskan wild fruits are typically far superior in antioxidant values and healthful constituents.

HIGHBUSH CRANBERRY
Viburnum edule
Adoxa family (Adoxaceae, formerly Honeysuckle, Caprifoliaceae)

Highbush cranberry shrub grows to 8 feet high. Its leaves are in an opposite arrangement along the stem (unlike currants, which alternate). The maple-like leaves are lobed except for the uppermost pair, which are linear. The white to pinkish flowers are in flat clusters, with individual tubular blossoms bearing 5 petals and 5 stamens. The tart fruits each contain 1 large flat stone. Taste a raw highbush cranberry, and you're apt to grimace. But vibrant highbush cranberry jelly and other related products are an absolute delight.

DERIVATION OF NAME: *Viburnum* is Latin for "wayfaring tree;" *edule* means "edible."

OTHER NAMES: highbush salmonberry, *uqpingnyaq* (Iñupiaq), *qalzakuaq* (Yupik), *kaxwéex* (Tlingit). *łáay* (Haida), *ttsuntsa* (Dena'ina).

RANGE: Southeast Alaska to the Alaska Peninsula and north to the Arctic; rare in westernmost and northernmost Alaska.

HARVESTING DIRECTIONS: Gather before frost for fruits with a fresh aroma and higher pectin content. Or harvest after frost, as chilling sweetens the fruits somewhat. Pick flowers in early summer. Harvest bark from pruned stems in fall to early spring.

FOOD USE: Add flowers or fruits to campfire hotcakes. The only raw highbush cranberries I truly savor are those found on winter expeditions; the frozen fruits have a refreshing natural sherbet quality that quenches thirst from cross-country skiing. Cooked fruits, run through a food mill, make tasty jellies and syrups. See the *Alaska Floats My Boat* blog (alaskafloatsmyboat.com) for a step-by-step guide to making delectable highbush cranberry ketchup.

HEALTH USE: In Southeast Alaska, Tlingit boiled the bark as external lotion for skin diseases. Alutiiq people mashed inner bark as a poultice for infected wounds. Other indigenous Alaskan uses range from using the stem as a steambath switch, to sipping highbush cranberry syrup to ease coughs, to drinking outer bark infusions for constipation as well as cold prevention. A Czech study of highbush cranberry noted its exceptional vitamin C content and antioxidant properties and concludes that consumption "can have a significant influence on strengthening human immunity and the prevention of many diseases." As indicated by the common name "crampbark," *Viburnum* species have long been used for relief of back, leg, stomach, and menstrual cramps, as well as cough spasms and asthma. *Viburnum* contains the antispasmodics scopoletin, aesculetin, and viburnin, which relax smooth muscles and peripheral blood vessels, plus the anti-inflammatory salicin. Due to the highbush cranberry's highly bitter nature, some people prefer a low dose alcohol or glycerin base tincture (½ to 1 teaspoon, 3 to 4 times a day) to drinking a cup of decoction 3 times a day.

OTHER: British Columbia Indians stored steamed, slightly underripe fruits in water in cedar boxes. Patch ownership was highly esteemed. Fresh fruits, as well as fruits preserved in water or eulachon grease, were widely traded along the northwest Canadian coast and from the coast to the Interior.

SALMONBERRY

Rubus spectabilis
Rose family (Rosaceae), Rose subfamily (Rosoideae)

FLOWER STAGE

FRUIT STAGE

"A rose by any other name would smell as sweet," penned Shakespeare. And for Alaskans, I'd say, "A salmonberry by any other name would taste as delicious." Depending where in Alaska you are, the common name salmonberry can refer to the tall *Rubus spectabilis* (addressed here) or to the petite *Rubus arcticus* (see cloudberry on page 110). There are also abundant Native names for this rose family shrub. Salmonberry canes bear weak spines, can soar to 7 feet in height, and often form dense thickets. Leaves are tri-foliate and toothed. The bright pink, early blooming flowers are a hummingbird favorite. The raspberry-like fruits are thumb sized and are red or orange-gold at maturity.

DERIVATION OF NAME: *Rubus* means "bramble;" *spectabilis* translates as "exceptionally showy."

OTHER NAMES: highbush salmonberry, *nquɫkegh* (Dena'ina, "cloudberry big"), *qiumalzaa/qategyataguaq* (Yup'ik, "red berry/yellow berry"), *sq'aw.aan* (Haida).

RANGE: Primarily a coastal species, ranging from Southeast to Southcentral Alaska and the Aleutian Islands.

HARVESTING DIRECTIONS: Salmonberry shoots are prime in spring. Pick salmonberry buds and blossoms as they appear in mid to late spring. Be sure to save plenty for summer harvest of ripe plump and juicy fruits.

FOOD USE: The Haida name *s'ixaal, ts'iixaal* translates as "edible shoots;" the peeled spring shoots are a delicacy. Nibble buds and blossoms or add as a garnish on spring salads. My favorite "salmonberry flower tea" evolved during a Wrangell wild plants class when students were exploring the effects of heat on a single herb. They contrasted salmonberry flowers steeped in cold water overnight versus steeping in hot water 10 minutes (herbal infusions or tea) versus simmering the flowers for 20 minutes (decoction). The cold-water floral infusion retained aroma and color and yielded a delectable sweet flavor. The hot infusion was a pleasant tea, somewhat closer to a black tea. The decoction was extremely astringent, making it far more suited as a "wound wash." Snack on fresh salmonberry fruits. Make salmonberry jam. Salmonberry pie. Salmonberry muffins. Salmonberry smoothies. Salmonberry vinegar. Salmonberry marinade for salmon. Salmonberry yogurt. Salmonberry liqueur. Eating salmonberries with salmon eggs or seal oil is a favorite in Native villages within its range.

HEALTH USE: Salmonberry leaves are an astringent poultice for burns and infected wounds. Decoctions of leaves, bark, and root ease diarrhea. Explorers drank the brew to settle intestinal upset. If you're camping and suffering from toothache, try applying the pounded root to relieve pain.

OTHER: Use the astringent leaves and root decoctions as a rinse for oily hair. In Tlingit culture, hunting grounds, fish streams, and berry patches are owned by particular clans. Salmonberry patches were an item of prestige, and picking rights were highly prized.

FIDDLEHEAD FERN

Dryopteris dilatata (shield fern), *Athyrium filix-femina* (lady fern),
Matteuccia struthiopteris (ostrich fern)
Wood fern family (Dryopteridaceae)

Fiddleheads, or croziers, are the coiled spring growth of ferns. Of particular interest to Alaskan foragers are shield, lady, and ostrich ferns. Ostrich fiddleheads are smooth at emergence, with a U-shaped groove on the inside of the stem, and bits of light papery chaff. Ostrich ferns mature with plume-shaped fronds and produce shorter central fronds that bear spores. Lady ferns also have plume-like fronds, while those of wood fern are triangular. Both wood and lady ferns have fiddleheads with brown woody chaff; spores are borne on the undersides of their green fronds.

> **DERIVATION OF NAME:** *Struthiopteris* means "ostrich feather"; *dryopteris* translates as "oak feather"; and *filix-femina* means "lady fern."
>
> **OTHER NAMES:** *ts'aagwaal* (Haida, *A. filix-femina*), *kw'álx* (Tlingit, "ferns with edible roots").

RANGE: From the Brooks Range southward to the Aleutian Islands and the Alaska Panhandle.

HARVESTING DIRECTIONS: Fiddleheads are prime when tightly coiled in early spring. Harvest no more than ¼ to ⅓ of the fiddleheads from each cluster to allow the plant to thrive. Snap fiddleheads close to the base as the young "fiddlesticks" are equally as good as the coiled croziers. Harvest season ends when the fern fronds begin to unfurl.

FOOD USE: Remove (and discard) chaff from fiddleheads (see Other below). Sauté fiddleheads in herb butter or olive oil. Pickle fiddleheads. Top pizza with fiddleheads. Serve fiddlehead soup, glazed salmon with fiddleheads, or marinated fiddleheads. Blanch fiddleheads, then chill and serve with a curry or herbal mayonnaise. Even finicky children love batter-dipped fried fiddleheads. For year-round use, can fiddleheads, or blanch 2 minutes and freeze.

HEALTH USE: Fiddleheads are excellent sources of vitamins A and C; minerals include calcium, magnesium, iron, manganese, and zinc.

OTHER: Everyone has their favorite way of cleaning fiddleheads. Some soak croziers in water and then drain and rub on a wire strainer set over a pot (letting chaff fall through). Others rub raw or parboiled fiddleheads in a clean dishtowel. Some soak them for half an hour in a basket or wire cage set in a fast-flowing stream. A forager's YouTube video demos placing raw fiddleheads in a sieve and holding over a fan to blow away the chaff. In *Tanaina Plantlore*, Priscilla Russell Kari reports that fall- or spring-gathered roots of *Dryopteris* and *Athyrium* were placed in holes in the ground and covered with coals to bake, and then peeled and eaten. In Southeast, *k'wálx xaadi* is Tlingit for fern root; both fiddleheads and roots were eaten, but definitive details on species used are unavailable at this time. Documentation is also lacking as to whether Alaska's shield fern's "roots" have similar properties to foreign species. In traditional Chinese medicine, the underground rootstock of *Dryopteris crassi* is used as a bitter antiparasitic herb for tapeworms, roundworms, and pinworms. Unless thoroughly cooked and taken within prescribed dosages, it can cause side effects including central nervous system disturbances, headaches, and miscarriage. Animals eating this shield fern rhizome raw have experienced transient or permanent blindness. Note that Natives always ate fern roots cooked, and cooking often deactivates many toxins.

CAUTION: Alaska Plant Materials Center warns: "Repeated overharvesting of the fiddleheads will eventually exhaust root nutrient reserves to the point of plant death." In Southeast Alaska, bracken fern (*Pteridium*) also grows; bracken fiddleheads emerge singly rather than in clusters and look more like an eagle's clenched talon. Bracken fern is toxic to many animal species. Whether to eat bracken is a personal decision. For now, I'm keeping to my trusty 3.

CHIMING BELLS
Mertensia paniculata
Borage family (Boraginaceae)

Chiming bells are in the same genus as oysterleaf (*Mertensia maritima* on page 56), but since these plants live in such different habitats (woodland versus beach) and have such different appearances, they score separate pages in this guide. Chiming bell leaves have hairy green leaves with a light cucumber-like taste, whereas bluish-grey smooth-leaf oysterleaf is reminiscent of, you guessed it, oysters. Both have pink buds that mature as blue tubular flowers. What the *Mertensias* and its garden family cousins comfrey and borage all have in common is the pattern of their bell-like flowers. Dissect one and you will notice that the 5 petals are all fused together, with stamens attached.

DERIVATION OF NAME: *Mertensia* honors the 19th-century German botanist Franz Karl Mertens; *paniculata* indicates that the flowers are in a botanical arrangement called panicles.

OTHER NAMES: bluebells, lungwort.

RANGE: Southcentral Alaska west to Bethel and north to the Brooks Range.

HARVESTING DIRECTIONS: Leaves are prime before flowering. Pick flowers when fully open, before petals fade.

FOOD USE: The reason chiming bells leaves are not more widely used is because of their hairy texture. I sometimes chop them finely and add them to salads, but they are best suited for cooked dishes. Add to campfire soups and stir-fries. Flowers are delightful in a multitude of ways: salad garnish, in gelatin salads, frozen into ice cubes or children's popsicles. Add fresh or dry flowers and leaves to beverage teas.

HEALTH USE: Lungwort is a common name for many *Mertensia* species, which were historically used in the treatment of whooping cough and other respiratory complaints.

OTHER: Like fireweed, chiming bells regenerate quickly following fire, softening the charred landscape with carpets of color. A Canadian clinical trial by Grainger and Turkington explored how plants respond to "burning of fossil fuels, inputs from industrial fertilizers and faster mineralization rates" resulting from global warming, which increases available nitrogen levels. In their study, plants like chiming bells and fireweed increased substantially, whereas yarrow population remained constant, and other species declined. "Experimental evidence from a variety of ecosystems including grasslands, temperate forests and arctic tundra has shown that nutrient enrichment leads to species loss when some species are out-competed to local extinction in the altered environment." Unless we address the root causes of rising global temperatures, we will continue to see dramatic shifts in plant communities around the world. Nitrogen-loving plants like chiming bells will prosper while others will perish.

CAUTION: Many plants in the borage family, including *Mertensia*, contain pyrrolizidine alkaloids and other constituents that can be hepatotoxic in large quantities. Use moderation.

TWISTED STALK

Streptopus amplexifolius

Lily family (Liliaceae), Sego lily subfamily (Calochortoideae)

Botanical names are often intimidating to new foragers, but essential to use if you seek additional information on a plant. Common names, even within a region, can vary dramatically. Some plant names honor the botanist who first described the plant. I particularly like the binomial *Streptopus amplexifolius* as it so definitively describes: "the twisted stalk with the clasping leaf." Notice that twisted stalk's greenish-white flowers also hang on distinctive kinked stalks. An even closer look reveals 6 tepals (3 pistils and 3 sepals of identical size and color) that curve back. Stamens number 6. The stem is kinked with alternating leaves that wrap around the stem at its base. Though the fruit registers the lowest of all Alaska's berries in antioxidant value (19 on ORAC scale compared to 206 for lingonberry), the plant is a good source of vitamins A and C. The fruits have a refreshing flavor with a hint of watermelon. Like prunes, they can help sluggish bowels to move, so be aware of how much you eat at one time (one common name is "scootberry").

DERIVATION OF NAME: *Streptopus amplexifolius* means "the twisted stalk with the clasping leaf."

OTHER NAMES: wild cucumber, watermelon berry, scootberry, liverberry.

RANGE: Southeast Alaska to the Aleutian Islands and northward to the Yukon River.

HARVESTING DIRECTIONS: Be mindful how much you harvest of the tender spring stalks (stem and leaves). I playfully threaten to flog students with stinging nettles if they don't leave enough for the plants to carry on their life cycle. Harvest the watery fruits in summer when plump and fully red.

FOOD USE: The young cucumber-flavored shoots are a delicious trail snack or addition to tossed salads. Fried as tempura, the flavor becomes quite similar to asparagus. The ripe watermelon-tasting berries can be nibbled fresh as a snack, juiced, processed into jelly or syrup, or added to muffins or breakfast cereal. In *Plant Lore of an Alaskan Island: Foraging in the Kodiak Archipelago*, Fran Kelso has a delightful recipe for shredded twisted stalk leaves and stems mixed with sweet onion, sugar (or mild honey), salt, pepper, and vinegar.

HEALTH USE: Tea of stems and fruits has traditionally been used as a general "tonic" due to its flavonoids and other nutrients. Be aware that excess of berries has the potential to trigger an enthusiastic release from the bowels. Moderation is the key.

CAUTION: I've often found twisted stalk growing side by side with deadly false hellebore (see page 179). Though the plants are dramatically different when in flower, some foragers have been confused during early spring phase. In addition, in the Turnagain Arm–Anchorage vicinity and in the southern Panhandle, the somewhat similar-looking but bitter-tasting and purgative false Solomon's seal (*Maianthemum*, formerly *Smilacina* spp.) occurs. Beloved botanist, the late Verna Pratt taught me that Solomon's seal lacks the black hairs on the lower stem that are characteristic of the choice edible twisted stalk.

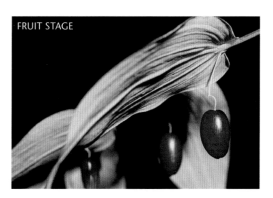

FRUIT STAGE

VIOLET
Viola species
Violet family (Violaceae)

PURPLE VIOLET   YELLOW VIOLET

Violets have been described as one of the most "underappreciated, important tonic herbs." Though violet flowers are recognized worldwide, their other sterling qualities are far less commonly known. The 5 irregular petals vary in hue from violet to snow-white and bright yellow. The wild violas are perennial. The heart-shaped leaves may rise from the base or alternate on the stems. Seeds are in 3-valved capsules.

DERIVATION OF NAME: *Viola* is said to be the Latin name for the Greek nymph Io. After Io was transformed into a cow, Zeus caused her tears to become violets.

OTHER NAMES: wild violet, Alaska violet, marsh violet, yellow violet.

RANGE: Throughout Alaska, except the extreme north Arctic.

HARVESTING DIRECTIONS: Selectively harvest leaves and flowers throughout the green season. Though most tender before bloom, leaves remain palatable throughout the summer.

FOOD USE: Add leaves and flowers to salads. Try violet flower vinegar. Violet wine. Violet syrup. Violet jelly. Violet leaf and flower tea. Candied violets are a stunning birthday cake decoration.

HEALTH USE: Diverse violet species have been used worldwide for easing ailments ranging from respiratory problems to skin cancers. Clinical trials of a violet syrup, published in *Science Direct*, concluded that its efficacy and safety "in treatment of pain, fever, cough, infection and inflammation may make it a suitable treatment for respiratory ailments." In an Iranian clinical trial, nasal drops of violet oil (2 drops in each nostril before bed) were demonstrated to ease chronic insomnia. Internally, violet leaves are a superior source of vitamin C (264 mg) and vitamin A (20,000 IU) per 100 g of fresh leaf. External applications of antiseptic mashed leaves soothe cuts, boils, and scrapes. Burned dry roots of marsh violet (*V. epipsela*) are used by Dena'ina Athabascans to purify rooms with fragrant perfume to ward off disease. Violet leaf is used by herbalists as a poultice for fibrous breasts and mastitis and as a low dose tincture (3 drops 3 times a day).

OTHER: Add violets to lotions to moisturize the skin. Cultivate violets for a backyard supply. The Alaska violet (*Viola langsdorffii*) is suited for growing in moist well-drained soils ranging from sandy to heavy clay. It prefers acid to neutral and can grow in semi-shade in light woodlands to open areas.

CAUTION: Violets, especially those that have more mucilaginous-tasting leaves (as in some yellow-flowered varieties) can have the effect of eating stewed prunes. Be mindful of how much you eat.

Tundra

Tundra includes the vast treeless regions of the Arctic, lushly carpeted with lingonberries, Labrador tea, and cloudberries, as well as dwarf shrubs, mosses, lichens, grasses, and sedges.

Tundra is estimated to cover 10% of the earth's surface. It includes both low-lying Arctic Tundra as well as alpine. All tundra, regardless of altitude or latitude, is characterized by low mean air temperature throughout the growing season. Alaska's tundra is sometimes described as a "cold desert." It is a place of very little snow or rain. Annual precipitation at Utqiagvik, on the tundra-covered coastal plain, is about 4 inches—much less than the annual rainfall of the Mojave Desert. The growing season above Alaska's Arctic Circle normally averages 50–60 days. Summer is a time of endless light, and many plants have adaptations like woolly hairs to cope with climatic challenges.

A major concern with present global warming is melting of the permafrost, as permafrost "contains about one and a half times the amount of carbon already in the atmosphere today, as well as large amounts of methane, another potent greenhouse gas," writes Christina Nunez in a National Geographic article. "As the permafrost melts and dead plant material decomposes and releases greenhouse gases, the tundra has flipped from a carbon sink to a carbon contributor."

TUNDRA

CLOUDBERRY
Rubus chamaemorus
Rose family (Rosaceae), Rose subfamily (Rosoideae)

Cloudberries are a perfect example of the confusion that can be caused by common names. In northern Alaska, these tiny jewels are commonly called salmonberry; in the southern regions, salmonberry is the tall shrubby *Rubus spectabilis*. Local cloudberry names include *aqpik, nqutl'*, baked appleberry, and ground mulberry (the translation of its specific name). Use whatever common name you prefer in your region, but do learn to recognize and use this raspberry relative. Cloudberry grows as high as your ankle and bears one 5-petaled white flower and 1 to 3 lobed toothed leaves per plant.

DERIVATION OF NAME: *Rubus* means "bramble"; *chamaemorus* translates as "ground mulberry."

OTHER NAMES: lowbush salmonberry, knotberry, *puyurniq* (Yupik), *néx'w* (Tlingit).

RANGE: Cloudberry ranges through arctic and alpine tundra, as well as peat bogs throughout Alaska.

HARVESTING DIRECTIONS: Pick the fruits when plump and yellow-orange to golden-red. Flowers are safe to eat, but fruits are generally preferred.

FOOD USE: Nibble cloudberries raw. Puree and dry as fruit leather. Blend in fruit smoothies. Process into jam or jelly. Combine with your favorite berries and top with yogurt as a simple nutritious dessert. For winter use, freeze berries. In *Plants That We Eat*, Anore Jones documents that Iñupiat preserve cloudberries in a barrel with sourdock, seal oil, or blackberries (crowberries) for winter storage; methods are fully detailed in her excellent guide. The berries contain the natural preservative benzoic acid.

HEALTH USE: The Cooperative Extension Service of Alaska notes that ⅔ cup of cloudberries contains 158 mg vitamin C (in comparison to a mere 9.7 mg in commercial blueberries); vitamin A is 210 IU compared to 54 IU. Cloudberries also contain vitamin E, and cell protective antioxidants. Use fruits and leaves as tea; they are a source of micronutrients and macronutrients including calcium, magnesium, zinc, and iron, as well as flavonoids and ellagic acid (antioxidants with antimicrobial and anticarcinogenic properties).

OTHER: Cloudberry liqueur is a Scandinavian favorite. Finnish cosmetic company Lumene is marketing an "Age Defying Arctic Cloudberry Nourishing Day Cream."

CROWBERRY

Empetrum nigrum
Heath family (Ericaceae), Heath subfamily (Ericoideae)

Crowberries—or blackberries, as they're commonly called in northern Alaska—have seedy blue-black fruits that grow on trailing stems in an evergreen carpet. The narrow, needle-like leaves have edges that roll back and meet. South of Anchorage, crowberries have separate male- and female-flowered plants, so if you happen upon a patch of "bachelors" you'll find yourself berryless. North of Anchorage, the flowers are bisexual, but you'll need a magnifying glass to appreciate their structure. A number of Alaska's plants, including crowberries (*Empetrum*), have recently been reclassified into the health family with blueberry due to DNA analysis revealing previously unknown genetic relationships.

DERIVATION OF NAME: *Empetrum* is from the Greek meaning "upon a rock"; *nigrum* means "black."

OTHER NAMES: mossberry, *pakik* (Yupik), *hidli wutsi* (Tlingit), *xoya gaan* (Haida, "raven's berry").

RANGE: Throughout Alaska.

HARVESTING DIRECTIONS: Fruits are sweeter after fall frosts. Place any summer-harvested fruits in the freezer to sweeten them. Pick overwintered fruits after snowmelt.

FOOD USE: Add antioxidant-rich crowberries to muffins and pancakes. Make crowberry jam. Crowberry jelly. Crowberry juice. Crowberry liqueur. Use dried berries in fruit-nut bars for the trail. Freeze, can, or dry crowberries for winter use; Alaska Natives often preserve their "blackberries" in seal oil. Iñupiat blend them with fish livers to make *tinulik. Agutuk*, a blend of berries and fat, is a favorite treat of indigenous Alaskans.

HEALTH USE: A clinical trial by Park and Lee on *Empetrum* demonstrated that taking 2 g of powdered crowberries daily for 4 weeks "led to significant increase in total antioxidant status" and "significant decrease in total cholesterol and low-density lipoprotein (LDL) levels." In a *Saudi Journal of Biological Sciences* study, the berries demonstrated antibacterial, antifungal, and anti-inflammatory effects. The leaves, stems, roots, and berries have a long history of use throughout Alaska in treating ailments ranging from stomach and intestinal upsets to kidney troubles. Dr. Robert Fortuine reported that "in the Kotzebue Sound area, crowberry juice was squeezed into the eye for cataract." Dena'ina Athabascans in the outer and upper Cook Inlet area used crowberry leaf and stem decoctions to remove a growth on an eye and to heal sore eyes.

OTHER: Crowberries are circumboreal, ranging throughout the northern region of the Northern Hemisphere. They also exist in the southernmost regions of South America. It is believed that this extreme range is due to migratory bird seed dispersal from the mid-Pleistocene era.

LINGONBERRY
Vaccinium vitis-idaea
Heath family (Ericaceae), Blueberry subfamily (Vaccinioideae)

Though in the same genus with blueberry, *Vaccinium vitis-idaea* bears fruits that are far more "cranberry" in taste. These diminutive shrubs are hardy evergreens that spread by underground stems. Lowbush cranberries are tolerant of Alaskan winter temperature extremes but are noted to be less productive in hot summers, thus climate change could potentially affect subsistence use of this treasured fruit. The tiny plants are sometimes confused with kinnikinnick (*Arctostaphylos uva ursi*). But look closely at the oval leaves with a magnifier. The underside of lingonberry leaves has characteristic dark dots, and the mature red fruits taste like cranberries. (*Uva ursi* leaves have pale undersides and fruits are bland, with a mealy texture.)

DERIVATION OF NAME: *Vaccinium* is the classical name for blueberry and cranberry; *vitis-idaea* means "vine of Mount Ida," honoring a mountain in Crete (today called Mount Idhi or Ìdhi Òros).

OTHER NAMES: lowbush cranberry, cowberry, rock cranberry, *dáx* (Tlingit).

RANGE: Throughout Alaska in moist acidic soil, tundra, boreal forests, and in the mountains to 3,000 feet.

HARVESTING DIRECTIONS: Gather lingonberries after fall frost. Overwintered fruits can often be found in spring.

FOOD USE: Grind lingonberries with oranges and walnuts, and sweeten with honey or maple syrup for a delicious holiday "cranberry" sauce. Dry and powdered berries are fabulous on Christmas cookies in place of red-dyed sugar. Add lingonberries to pancakes and nut breads. Lingonberry gravy is superb with wild game, and lingonberry sauce delectable on Alaskan salmon. Lingonberry jam is a centuries-old favorite, as is lingonberry liqueur. Fresh or dry lingonberries make a delicious tea. For a beverage concentrate that keeps well in the refrigerator, heat lingonberries slowly in a pan with honey and a few drops of water until berries "pop;" use 1 teaspoon concentrate per cup boiling water for a refreshing drink. The fruits contain benzoic acid, a natural preservative responsible for their outstanding keeping qualities.

HEALTH USE: Diverse Alaskan indigenous groups use lowbush cranberries for colds, sore throat, low energy, and urinary tract infections. Mashed fruits are used as a poultice to ease rashes. Lingonberry juice is a popular Scandinavian remedy to aid digestion. The fruits were used by Cree Indians in Quebec to treat diabetic symptoms. A Canadian clinical trial on mice confirmed that lingonberry exhibited antidiabetic activities in diet-induced obesity.

OTHER: In Soldotna, I listened to Dena'ina Athabascan elder Peter Kalifornsky speak of a young man left in the woods to hone his survival skills. The fellow only knew how to eat berries. He ate salmonberries and watermelon berries and cloudberries and crowberries but kept growing weaker and weaker. Finally, he turned to lingonberries and regained his strength. Lingonberries are indeed the most nutritious of all Alaskan berries. As reported in an *International Journal of Circumpolar Health study*, the ORAC (antioxidant) scale ranged from a low of 19 for watermelon berries to astounding 206 for lingonberries! The wisdom of the elders is once again confirmed by science.

LABRADOR TEA

Rhododendron tomentosum (formerly *Ledum palustre*),
Rhododendron groenlandicum (formerly *Ledum groenlandicum*)
Heath family (Ericaceae), Heath subfamily (Ericoideae),
Rhododendron tribe (Rhodoreae)

Though Labrador tea has been used for healing purposes by indigenous people for eons, the concept of using it as a "beverage tea" is believed to have been introduced to Alaskan and Canadian Natives by Russians and trappers. The leaf shape is quite similar to the toxic bog rosemary (*Andromeda polifolia*). But crush a leaf and Labrador tea wafts an enchanting scent. Look closely and you'll see that Labrador tea has felty, brownish undersides. Bog rosemary, on the other hand, lacks any distinct scent and has leaves with smooth, whitish undersides. When in flower, identity is even easier. Labrador tea has fragrant clusters of 5-petaled white blossoms. See Andromeda's pink bells on page 181 for comparison.

DERIVATION OF NAME: *Rhododendron* is from the Greek *rhodos* and *dendron*, meaning "rose tree."

OTHER NAMES: marsh tea, trapper's tea, Hudson Bay tea.

RANGE: Throughout Alaska except for the Aleutians.

HARVESTING DIRECTIONS: Though I generally pick green summer leaves and blossoms, some foragers prefer the brown winter leaves for tea.

FOOD USE: Use Labrador tea leaves in marinades for meat or fish. In soups, use *Ledum* leaves as a bay leaf substitute. In Nome, Alaska, Grace Johnson introduced me to the practice of combining Labrador tea with black tea to enhance flavor. Explorer Samuel Hearne reported in the 1770s that Labrador tea was "much used by the lower class of the [Hudson's Bay] Company's servants as tea; and by some is thought very pleasant. But the flower is by far the most delicate, and if gathered at the proper time, and carefully dried in the shade, will retain its flavor for many years and make a far more pleasant beverage than the leaves."

HEALTH USE: Dena'ina Athabascans drink *Ledum* infusions for heartburn, tuberculosis, colds, arthritis, and stomach problems. Yup'ik Natives sip boiled Labrador tea for food poisoning and upset stomach. My personal experience with the remedy occurred after too much Thanksgiving indulgence; my neighbor (a former resident in a Yup'ik village) guided me outdoors and we collected the winter-brown Labrador tea leaves by flashlight and boiled the leaves half an hour until a black brew resulted. One cup later, my system was "purged," so beware strong decoctions unless you specifically desire this body-cleansing effect. Note that small amounts of infused Labrador tea can help ease diarrhea, whereas larger decocted amounts can be laxative and/or purgative.

OTHER: Add leaves to potpourris and sachets to repel moths. Teas or tinctures are used for *external* application for lice, bedbugs, and other vermin. Labrador tea homeopathic (*Ledum*) is a staple in my wilderness first aid kit; it is specific for puncture wounds (and preventing tetanus).

CAUTION: Labrador tea leaves and flowers contain ledol, a narcotic toxin that can cause drowsiness, cramps, and heart palpitations. Ledol is reported not water soluble (thus, tea in moderate amounts is safely used). However, it's suggested that those with heart problems and high blood pressure consult their doctor before ingesting. The narcotic ledol from Labrador tea *does* extract readily in alcohol. In *Sacred and Herbal Healing Beers*, Stephen Buhner details Labrador tea's historical use in making beer more inebriating but warns that excess can trigger headaches, rage, delirium, and other nasty effects.

Meadows

I grew up in New Hampshire, the second-most forested state in the nation. Meadows were predominantly a manmade phenomenon. When I moved to Homer, Alaska, I was astounded by the abundance of naturally occurring grassy meadows ablaze with columbine, fireweed, and showy wildflowers. Such habitat is a place of both beauty and bounty for foragers.

BURNET

Sanguisorba species
Rose family (Rosaceae), Rose subfamily (Rosoideae)

EDIBLE STAGE   FLOWER STAGE

Young burnet has fan-like leaves in a pinnate arrangement. The fragrant blossoms look like baby bottlebrushes and may be greenish-white (Sitka burnet, *Sanguisorba stipulata*) or purplish (European burnet, *S. officinalis*, and hybrid *S. Menziesii*). European burnet is renowned as a salad herb, but very young Sitka burnet is a palatable substitute.

DERIVATION OF NAME: *Sanguisorba* is from the Latin *sangis*, "blood," and *sorbeo*, "to stop."

OTHER NAMES: Alaskan bottlebrush, bloodwort.

RANGE: European burnet, *S. officinalis*, ranges primarily from Denali north to the Brooks Range and on the Seward Peninsula; other species predominate from Southeast to the Alaska Peninsula and north to Denali.

HARVESTING DIRECTIONS: Pick leaves for food in early spring. Young burnet has a distinctive fan-like appearance and is most palatable at this stage. Once burnet flowers, the greens become far more astringent. (Astringent plants are great for stopping bleeding as they dry secretions. But they are unpleasant to eat as they make your mouth drier and drier.)

FOOD USE: Add spring burnet leaves to salads and dressings. Blend with other wild greens in spring rolls, casseroles, and soups.

HEALTH USE: Young greens are high in vitamins A and C. In Nicholas Culpeper's classic *Complete Herbal* (1653), he extols burnet for "preserving the body in health and the spirit in vigor." Burnet gatherers benefit from fresh air and exercise in foraging, as well as health-enhancing antioxidants (flavonoids quercetin and rutin). Burnet has styptic properties, i.e. it constricts tissues and seals damaged blood vessels. Gayla Pedersen of Kodiak reports applying crushed burnet leaves to the wound of an elder on blood thinners. He told her that normally it would have taken 2 hours to stop the bleeding, but with the burnet poultice it stopped within 5 minutes. In a Hong Kong clinical trial on European burnet, *S. officinalis* was shown to induce phase arrest and cell death in breast cancer cells. Researchers also noted the herb's anti-inflammatory and immunity-enhancing properties, and recommended additional research.

OTHER: *L'insalata non e buona ne bella, ove non e la pimpinella.* This Italian proverb translates as "Salad is neither good not pretty, that has no Pimpinella." Pimpinella is an old Italian name for salad burnet (*Sanguisorba minor*). Propagate burnet by seed or root division. Growing burnet in your own garden will allow you to observe it in all stages of growth and will provide a source of early spring greens. Burnet wine is reputed to cheer the spirits and drive away depression.

CHOCOLATE LILY
Fritillaria camschatcensis
Lily family (Liliaceae)

Giving bouquets of chocolate lilies to unsuspecting recipients is a favorite joke of children. These brown lilies are beautiful to behold, but surprise! Sniff deeply. The blossoms have a manure-like odor. Leaves are arranged in 2 to 3 whorls of 6 leaves, though first-year plants bear a single leaf. The underground corms have distinctive white rice-like kernels.

DERIVATION OF NAME: *Fritillaria* means "dice-box," referring to the seed capsule shape; *camschatcensis* refers to Kamchatka in Russia, where the corms were eaten by Natives.

OTHER NAMES: riceroot, Indian rice, wild rice.

RANGE: Southeast and Southcentral Alaska to the easternmost Aleutian Islands.

HARVESTING DIRECTIONS: Dig corms in late summer to early fall, when foliage is yellow, indicating that the plant's energy has returned to the corm, storing sugars and starches. Return a few rice-like kernels from each bulb to the earth to replant chocolate lily. I'd always hesitated harvesting chocolate lilies, not wanting to diminish my backyard patch, until after the summer of the plague of voles. The rodents sloppily dropped rice-like segments en route to their caches, and the following summer was a meadow of delight.

FOOD USE: Corms are bitter unless harvested late in the season. I enjoy them steamed or stir-fried with other more plentiful vegetables and topped with peanut sauce. Dena'ina Athabascans soak the corms in changes of water to remove any bitterness, and then boil their "wild rice" (in Dena'ina language, *qinazdli*). They typically serve the boiled corms with fish eggs or seal oil, or in soups. Traditionally, bulbs are dried and ground as a flour extender.

HEALTH USE: Various *Fritillaria* species have been used in traditional Chinese medicine for thousands of years, including Chuan Bei Mu, specific for dry coughs with difficulty expectorating. Subhuti Dharmananda, PhD, Director of the Institute for Traditional Medicine, Portland, Oregon, remarks, "In China, fritillaria is known as a safe herb that can be used in food preparations (such as fritillaria-pear) and for which there are no expected adverse reactions." To date, I've found no recorded medicinal use within Alaska.

EDIBLE CORM

COLUMBINE
Aquilegia formosa (red columbine), *A. brevistyla* (blue columbine)
Buttercup family (formerly Crowfoot family, Ranunculaceae)

Columbines bear showy red or purple flowers with nectar-filled spurs. Stems grow to 3 feet high from a brown carrot-like taproot. There may be 3 leaflets per basal stem (red columbine) or 1 leaflet with 3 deep lobes (purple columbine). Columbine grows easily from seed, which can be collected from the papery capsules.

DERIVATION OF NAME: *Aquilegia* may derive from the Latin *aqua*, "water," and *legere*, "collect," referring to the floral spur tips that contain sweet nectar water; or possibly from *aquila* for resemblance to an eagle's claw.

OTHER NAMES: granny's bonnet, dove's foot, *dall-sgid* (Haida, "red rain leaves/medicine").

RANGE: Southeast and Southcentral Alaska to the eastern Interior.

HARVESTING DIRECTIONS: Selectively pick flowers in summer when fully open, leaving abundant blooms to propagate the plant. Harvest seeds for sowing from the late summer or autumn capsules.

FOOD USE: Native children (and kids of all ages) suck on the nectar-filled spurs for a sweet treat. Scatter edible blossoms on your salads to delight your senses. Sprinkle columbine blooms (together with wild violets and wild rose petals, etc.) on halibut or salmon as a colorful and edible garnish.

HEALTH USE: In British Columbia, Natives applied columbine poultices for relief of respiratory congestion, muscular aches, and rheumatic joints. Pulverized columbine seed macerated with olive oil is reputed to be effective for lice.

OTHER: Columbine is commonly featured in religious paintings, to represent the seven gifts of the Holy Spirit. The plants are a striking addition to your wildflower garden and attract hummingbirds. As an Alaska flower essence, columbine is said to enhance self-appreciation. Omaha Indians used seeds as an aphrodisiac love charm. Hand a bouquet of lovely columbine blossoms to your sweetie, and see what magic unfolds.

CAUTION: Roots and seeds contain a cyanogenic glycoside and can cause poisoning if used internally. Seeds can be fatal to children. Though flowers are safely eaten, moderation is advised. Kidney or liver inflammation is possible from excessive intake.

COW PARSNIP

Heracleum lanatum, aka subspecies *H. sphondylium*, aka *H. maximum*
Parsley family (Apiaceae, formerly Umbelliferae)

Even though cow parsnip is, according to the *Journal of Ethnobiology*, "one of the most important of all indigenous green vegetables, in terms of the cultural and geographical extent of its use and the quantities consumed," it is condemned in numerous guides and online articles as poisonous. It is true that some individuals are highly allergic to it and that it can definitely rap you severely if you don't respect it. *Heracleum* is the major cause of contact dermatitis in Alaska. But it does have uses for the knowledgeable and nonallergic. Physically, this plant is of Herculean proportions, growing 6 to 8 feet high. Though in the same family as the deadly poison water hemlock (*Cicuta*), it would take profound lack of observational skills to confuse it. Cow parsnip's mature leaves are the size of dinner plates. Stems are stout, hollow, and woolly-hairy. From a central stem emerges umbrella-like spokes, each bearing a second umbrella (double umbel). The outer floral petals are noticeably longer than the inner petals.

DERIVATION OF NAME: *Heracleum* honors Hercules; *lanatum* means "woolly."

OTHER NAMES: wild celery, *pushki*, *pootschki*, Indian celery, *gis* (Dena'ina).

RANGE: Southeast Alaska to the Aleutians and north to the Yukon River.

HARVESTING DIRECTIONS: Use gloves and a knife to collect the stalks before flowering. Tlingit prefer plants growing in indirect sun and close to saltwater. Take your cut plants indoors or into a shady area to prepare. Scrape and discard the woolly covering on the stems. Proper preparation techniques reduce potential toxicity. It is essential that the entire outer skin (epidermis plus fibrous tissue) of the stalk be removed (similar to peeling rhubarb) or you can experience burns or blisters. Wash hands well after handling.

FOOD USE: Alaska Natives often eat the plant raw, dipped in seal oil. I've used peeled young stems as a celery substitute in wilderness soups, and in dishes ranging from stir-fries and egg rolls to casseroles. The young peeled stem can be sliced thinly, blanched, and frozen for winter use. Though Lower 48 field guides often tout the root as a parsnip substitute, my attempts to eat the roots failed spectacularly. Despite multiple methods of preparation ranging from twice-boiled to baked, my conclusion was that the root tasted like a worming medicine. (Dena'ina Athabascans, in fact, used small bits of raw root in meat to deworm dogs.)

HEALTH USE: Externally, heated mashed roots are applied as a poultice for arthritic pain. New Mexico herbalist Michael Moore advocated 1 teaspoon dry cow parsnip root in 1 cup water for nausea, acid indigestion, and heartburn. For seasickness, seeds can be used in tincture or directly chewed. While at an Alaskan winter potluck years ago, a guest experienced severe stomach cramps. I went outdoors with a flashlight seeking an herbal helper. Cow parsnip umbels still containing seeds rose above the deep snow. A few sips of the seed tea provided dramatic relief. In clinical trials, cow parsnip root was demonstrated to have antifungal, antibacterial, and antiviral properties.

CAUTION: Inhaling the smoke from burning stalks can result in internal blisters and death. People weed whacking cow parsnip on summer days while wearing shorts have suffered extreme dermatitis. *Heracleum* species contain furanocoumarins, which, in the presence of sunlight, form complexes with DNA in human epidermis; handling the plants can trigger severe blistering and hyperpigmentation. Treatments for these blisters are varied, from steroid creams to jewelweed juice, aloe vera, vinegar and water, or homeopathic *Heracleum*. Gayla Pederson of Kodiak reports that plantain greatly reduced the blistering effect if applied immediately as a poultice. Some individuals are allergic to the plant even when it is properly handled. The plant should not be consumed by infants or pregnant women.

ELDER
Sambucus racemosa
Adoxa family (Adoxaceae, formerly Honeysuckle, Caprifoliaceae)

FLOWER STAGE   FRUIT STAGE

Elderberries are attractive shrubs bearing 5 to 7 odd-pinnate leaves; the woody stems are filled with a pithy foam-like core. The blossom clusters are yellowish-white when young; they are sometimes dubbed "Alaskan lilacs." The bright red "elderberries" have edible pulp but cyanide-containing seeds.

DERIVATION OF NAME: *Sambucus* is derived from the *sambuke*, a Greek musical instrument made from the hollow woody stem of elder; *racemosa* refers to the type of flower clusters (racemes).

OTHER NAMES: red elder, tree of music, *yéeł* (Tlingit), *akutaq* (Yupik).

RANGE: Southeast and Southcentral Alaska to the Alaska Peninsula.

HARVESTING DIRECTIONS: Gather flowers promptly after emergence, when yellowish-white. Dried at this stage for tea, they will retain a light color. (More mature, fully white flowers turn an unattractive black when dried.) Harvest summer fruits only when they are fully red.

FOOD USE: Add chopped fresh blossoms to pancake, waffle, and cake batters. Elderflower tempura-battered blossoms (fried until golden) are a special treat. Use blossoms to make syrup, lemonade, cordials, liqueurs, and elderflower mead (honey wine). Elderflowers are a favorite addition to my probiotic (non-alcoholic) "ginger beer." Red elderberry jelly has been sold commercially by Homer's Alaska Wild Berry Products. Berries must be used in a manner that removes the toxic seeds (via a food mill or straining through a jelly bag). A Homer friend made a fruit syrup concentrate for "fruit punch" for her family. When processing berries, use a well-ventilated area or headaches can result.

HEALTH USE: Sip elderflower tea as a nutritive tonic and for comfort during a cold. Elderflowers contain bioflavonoids, omega-3 and omega-6 fatty acids, and vitamins from A to E. *Sambucus* species flowers have been clinically demonstrated to have "diaphoretic, anticatarrhal, expectorant, diuretic, and anti-inflammatory actions," as reported in a Czech journal. The European Medicines Agency recommends them for upper respiratory infections. Blossom extracts demonstrated strong antibacterial effects on *E. coli*, MRSA, and *Staphylococcus aureus*. The flowers also contain phytoestrogens, plant substances hypothesized to have protective effects from developing prostate and breast cancer; elderflower tea is an herbal support for women experiencing menopausal symptoms.

OTHER: With climate change, red elderberries are maturing earlier in Alaska, and coinciding with salmon spawning. On Kodiak Island, researchers have found that brown bears are preferring elderberries to their traditional salmon. You can purchase expensive elderflower "anti-aging" skin products or make your own luscious elder blossom lotions for moisturizing your face, and soothing wrinkles or stretch marks. Add *Sambucus* leaves to insect repellent oils.

CAUTION: Only elder flowers and mature deseeded fruits are safe for consumption. Cyanide-inducing glycosides are contained in elder seeds, stems, roots, and immature fruits. Though stems are made into whistles as well as hollow pegs for tapping birch, the spongy pith in the stem's center must be thoroughly removed and stems boiled or dried thoroughly, or poisoning can result.

FIELD MINT
Mentha arvensis
Mint family (Lamiaceae, formerly Labiatae)

Mint, like mustard, is another classic plant for learning family pattern identification and teaching sensory awareness. Close your eyes and feel the plant. Square stems? Simple opposite leaves? Yes? Now smell the bruised plant. Field mint emits a delightful minty aroma. Open your eyes and observe closely. Mint has tubular flowers with united petals with 2 long and 2 short stamens. The lilac-colored flowers grow in a whorl where the leaves meet the stem.

DERIVATION OF NAME: *Mentha* is named after the Greek nymph Mintho, who was turned into a mint plant by Pluto's jealous wife, Proserpine. *Arvensis* means "pertaining to cultivated fields."

OTHER NAMES: wild mint, pole mint, brook mint, Indian mint.

RANGE: Throughout Southeast, western, and interior Alaska, with sporadic occurrences elsewhere. Greet mint in global travels from North America to the Himalayas and eastern Siberia.

HARVESTING DIRECTIONS: Clip mint tips in late spring, before flowering, and repeatedly throughout the growing season. Mint will vigorously keep producing new growth. Flowers are also useful. For year-round use, hang bundles of mint in a warm shady place upside down. When dry, strip leaves and store in an airtight container out of sunlight.

FOOD USE: Add young leaves and mint flowers to spring salads and salad dressings. Enjoy hot mint or cold mint tea, mint julep, or mint ginger beer as a midday refresher. Serve mint jelly with wild game. Make mint syrup. Put a few mint leaves in your baking pan before pouring in banana bread batter.

HEALTH USE: Leaves are high in vitamins A, C, and K and iron, calcium, and manganese. Sip a cup of mint tea if menstruation is delayed or crampy, or if you're suffering minor stomach upset. Try mint for alleviating seasickness. Clear your sinuses by placing your face over a steaming bowl of mint tea and inhaling deeply. Soothe your headache with a cool mint compress. Add a few drops essential oil of mint to salves and massage oils to ease muscle spasms. In clinical trials on rats suffering aspirin-induced ulcers, field mint was demonstrated to have a protective effect in reducing stomach ulcers.

OTHER: Sweaty after hiking? Splash mint tea on your body as a refreshing wash and natural deodorant. Add mint to herbal baths and footbaths. Field mint is a source of menthol essential oil used in the pharmaceutical and flavor industries. Stick a few sprigs of mint in water to sprout roots. Plant in a window box or container unless you want mint to spread throughout your herb garden.

CAUTION: Some individuals are allergic to mint. The *American Family Physician* lists mint essential oil as unsuited for those with "hiatal hernia, severe gastroesophageal reflux, gallbladder disorders; use with caution in pregnant and lactating women." They advocate enteric-coated capsules of mint when used internally. These cautions apply to essential oil of mint, which is highly concentrated, rather than whole plant in tea or food.

FIREWEED

Chamerion angustifolium (formerly *Epilobium angustifolium*)
Evening primrose family (Onagraceae)

Fireweed is the floral emblem of the Yukon and could easily be Alaska's too due to its extreme abundance. Fireweed's showy flowers have 4 petals each and vary in hue from bright pink to white. Lower flowers mature first; the blooming of the uppermost blossoms is said to portend the end of summer. Leaves are long, narrow, and willow-like.

DERIVATION OF NAME: I've always loved how fireweed's former genus name *Epilobium* ("upon a pod") so aptly described its mature stage, when the long seedpods opened cradling the down-laden seeds. Now, botanists have renamed it *Chamerion*, from the Greek meaning "near the ground," which doesn't describe this 3-foot-high herb at all. They consider this genus more appropriate due to morphological distinctions.

OTHER NAMES: willowherb, willow weed, blooming sally, wild asparagus.

RANGE: Throughout Alaska except the far northern tip.

HARVESTING DIRECTIONS: Pick the reddish, asparagus-like early spring shoots before the leaves develop; discard the strong-tasting tip (the uppermost inch), but do retain the white, blanched underground base. Pick young leaves as they emerge. Collect flowers when fully opened.

FOOD USE: Steam baby fireweed shoots as an asparagus substitute, or fry as tempura. Add a few spring leaves to soups, casseroles, and quiche. Pickle unopened buds as a capers substitute. Blossoms brighten tossed salads and yield delicious jelly. Children (and adults) like to split the summer stem and drag it through their teeth to extract the sweet pith. My favorite fireweed tea, introduced to me by a student, is Kapor tea, aka Ivan-chai. Forager Frank Shaw describes this tasting "very much like black tea, only with a fruity, almost pineapple-like aroma...and no caffeine." Full directions on making this "fermented tea" can be found on Joybilee Farm's blog (joybileefarm.com/fireweed-tea).

HEALTH USE: Spring fireweed shoots are high in vitamins A and C, as well as mucilage. Mucilage is a thick, slippery substance that extracts profusely when chopped young shoots are steeped in cold water overnight. The viscous cold infusions make a good gargle for soothing a scratchy throat or mouth ulcer. Or drink a cup to lubricate bowels and relieve constipation. Hot water infusions of fireweed leaves, on the other hand, are astringent and help tighten too loose bowels. Infusions and extracts of flowering tops are used in Europe for inhibiting Candida. Add leaves, flowers, and powdered root to salves and boluses for bleeding piles. Root poultices are traditional to draw infection from wounds, and to heal skin ulcers, including the hard-to-heal diabetic variety. In a clinical trial, whole plant fireweed extract inhibited growth of both Gram-positive and Gram-negative bacteria (including *Staphylococcus* and *E. coli*) more effectively than tetracycline.

OTHER: Fireweed regenerates soils after forest fires. The Alaskan fireweed floral essence is specific for those feeling "burned out" or suffering from trauma. River beauty (*Chamerion latifolium*, formerly *Epilobium latifolium*) is a smaller species common on gravel bars throughout Alaska that is also edible and reputed to have anti-inflammatory, antihistamine actions.

EDIBLE SHOOT

GERANIUM
Geranium erianthum
Geranium family (Geraniaceae)

An online site that ranks wild plants on an edibility scale gave *Geranium* species a ranking of 1, an indicator of being the least desirable. I can't honestly disagree. The leaves aren't sensational, even when "most prime" in spring. And at that stage you need a very sharp eye to positively distinguish them from deadly monkshood leaves. When in flower, however, the plants are highly distinctive and very abundant south of the Brooks Range. In Alaska, where so many people explore the wild and can suffer scrapes and scratches, wild geranium is a very good plant to know. Geranium has 5 green sepals, and showy purple 5-petaled blossoms with dark purple stripes. Leaves are palmate, with the upper ones sessile (lacking stems) and the lower ones on long stems. Leaves are remarkably similar in shape to deadly monkshood, so be absolutely positive of identity before taking a nibble. Geranium leaves are slightly rough and hairy. Observe the buds and you'll notice downy hairs.

DERIVATION OF NAME: The *Geranium* name is from the Greek *geranos*, "crane," referring to the "cranesbill" that develops after the flower petals drop off; this beak-like "schizocarp" splits apart and forcibly flings the seeds for dispersal.

OTHER NAMES: cranesbill, sticky geranium, stork's bill.

RANGE: Southeast and Southcentral Alaska to the Aleutians and north to Unalakleet and Denali National Park.

HARVESTING DIRECTIONS: Harvest geranium blossoms when newly opened.

FOOD USE: Geranium flowers are colorful for salads, flatbreads, dips, potato salad, and frosted cakes. When I lived in the bush, wild geraniums grew abundantly outside my door and I used very young leaves in soups and casseroles to stretch supplies of more delectable greens like goosetongue and spring beauty.

HEALTH USE: Have a toothache out in the bush? New Mexico herbalist Michael Moore recommended using the freshly sliced root for gum or tooth infection; apply directly to the painful area. Use root power in suppositories for bleeding hemorrhoids. Roots are astringent and decocted for diarrhea and dysentery. Mrs. Grieve in *A Modern Herbal* adds: "the leaves are also used and give the greatest percentage of tannin and should be collected before the plant seeds." Mexican clinical trials of numerous *Geranium* species documented them to be promising hepatoprotective agents for alcohol-induced liver damage as well as antiviral and anti-inflammatory agents.

OTHER: If you're feeling lethargic and indecisive, you could try a floral essence of Sticky Geranium as a helper for getting unstuck and becoming more decisive and focused (alaskanessences.com/products/sticky-geranium-i-geranium-erianthum-i).

CAUTION: Geranium leaves can be confused with those of deadly monkshood (*Aconitum delphinifolium* on page 178). Both geraniums and monkshood bear palmate leaves, which are divided into 5 lobed parts. Monkshood tend to be more finely divided but plants can vary. Study both throughout the seasons so that you can differentiate at all stages.

Monkshood (left), Geranium (right).

GOLDENROD

Solidago species
Aster family (Asteraceae, aka Compositae),
Aster subfamily, Aster tribe (Astereae)

Alaska's 5 goldenrod species collectively range throughout Alaska, frequenting meadows and open woods and ranging in the mountains to 3,000 feet. *Solidago multiradiata* is most widespread. Goldenrod bears showy clusters of golden blossoms containing both ray and disk flowers (characteristic of composite flowers). Stems grow 2 to 3 feet high and have alternate leaves with smaller upper-stem leaves. Leaf teeth are typically sharp or rounded (the uncommon *S. canadensis* can have leaves with smooth edges). Goldenrod is most easily recognized when in flower; return to your favorite patch to learn it in all seasons. (See Caution on the next page.)

DERIVATION OF NAME: *Solidago* means "to make whole," referring to its reputation as a healing herb.

OTHER NAMES: woundwort, Aaron's rod.

RANGE: Throughout Alaska.

HARVESTING DIRECTIONS: Harvest leaves for food before buds form (discard any insect-damaged leaves). Collect flowers for beverage use when at their peak in mid to late summer, stripping flowers from the stem. Gather the flowering top for teas (flower and leaf) just before the peak of bloom. Harvest seeds late summer to early autumn.

FOOD USE: Flowers are my favorite goldenrod product, yielding a golden beverage tea; sweeten with a dab of honey as desired. Flowers, infused in apple cider or rice vinegar for a month, then strained, yield a lovely tonic herb vinegar. Goldenrod was abundant in my cabin's meadow, and a frequent ingredient in my "wild green blends" for quiche, soups, and casseroles. Though leaves are not overwhelmingly delectable on their own, they are good to stretch food supplies. Flowers featured in pancakes, as well as in my ever-changing seasonal beverage blend that I dubbed "Night on Rocky River Tea." I've yet to sample using seeds in stews as a thickener.

HEALTH USE: Mash leaves and apply as a poultice to insect bites and stings. Alutiiq people use goldenrod as a steambath switch to relieve muscular aches and cramps; they applied goldenrod poultices on a woman's abdomen to ease menstrual cramps. Goldenrod teas, syrups, and tinctures are traditional herbal remedies for strengthening the kidneys, soothing urinary inflammations and kidney stones, and reducing bronchial congestion. A German abstract published in *Wiener Medizinische Wochenschrift* notes that goldenrod's "complex action spectrum (anti-inflammatory, antimicrobial, diuretic, antispasmodic, analgesic) is especially recommended for treatment of infections and inflammations, to prevent formation of kidney stones and to help remove urinary gravel. This therapy is safe at a reasonable price and does not show drug-related side-effects."

OTHER: Herbalists at Red Moon Herbs suggest goldenrod flowers "as an aromatic steambath/mist for clogged sinuses and cold/flu" and a circulatory-stimulating footbath.

CAUTION: Be positive of identity as there are abundant DYCs (darn yellow composites) in Alaska and not all are safe to ingest. Check resources like Verna's Pratt's photo field guides and online sites like wildflowers-and-weeds.com to learn to differentiate potential lookalikes.

NAGOONBERRY
Rubus arcticus
Rose family (Rosaceae), Rose subfamily (Rosoideae)

FLOWER STAGE

FRUIT STAGE

Nagoonberry is eye level to a mouse but of interest to far more than rodents. The flowers are an eye-catching hot pink. Leaves may be partially or fully divided into 3 lobes. Fruits are red, made up of many drupelets resembling small raspberries (to which they are related).

DERIVATION OF NAME: "Arctic bramble" is the translation of *Rubus arcticus*; the common name nagoonberry is from the Tlingit *neigóon*, *néegúun*, meaning "little jewels that pop from the ground." The Dena'ina Athabascan names *nughuya giga* and *nughuya nqitł'a* translate to "frog's berry" and "frog's cloudberry."

OTHER NAMES: Arctic raspberry, *pururniq* (Yupik), *knyazhenika* (Russian, "the berry of princes").

RANGE: From Southeast Alaska to the Aleutians.

HARVESTING DIRECTIONS: Pick the flowers at their peak, before petals begin to wither. Gather fruits when sweet and soft; selectively gather leaves when green.

FOOD USE: Nagoonberry blossoms are a sweet trail nibble. Add fresh or dried fruits and leaves to beverage teas. Nagoonberries are delectable but difficult to gather in quantity. Iñupiat Eskimos use *Rubus arcticus* to heighten flavor of the more abundant *R. chamaemorus*.

HEALTH USE: Nagoonberries, like other *Rubus* fruits, are a source of bioactive antioxidants that scavenge free radicals. Leaves and roots are astringent; decoctions are a wash for wilderness cuts, scratches, and mosquito bites. Fruits are extremely high in vitamins A and C.

OTHER: Nagoonberries make a superior jelly; in the early 1970s, the berries were marketed by an Alaskan preserve company for $45 pint. In Estonia, they have been a protected species since 1958, a relic of subarctic conditions. Experiments are being done in Scandinavia to cultivate nagoonberries. Mesimarja is an aromatic Finnish alcohol that contains nagoonberry.

MEADOWS

RASPBERRY
Rubus idaeus
Rose family (Rosaceae), Rose subfamily (Rosoideae)

Rubus is a complex genus, ranging from the diminutive nagoonberries and cloudberries to the familiar red raspberry. *Rubus* species are native on all continents—except Antarctica—in habitats from sea level to alpine. Wild raspberries are the same species as the garden variety. They thrive on bristly stems that can reach 6 feet high. Leaflets have irregular teeth and number 3 to 5. Flowers are white with 5 petals. The berries themselves need little description, being such a common household fruit.

DERIVATION OF NAME: *Rubus* means red or bramble; *idaeus* translates as "of Mount Ida."

OTHER NAMES: wild raspberry, framboise, *tłéiq yádi* (Tlingit), *nuqłkegh* (Dena'ina, "cloudberry big").

RANGE: Southeast to Southcentral Alaska and north to the Yukon River.

HARVESTING DIRECTIONS: For tea, harvest tender new leaf growth throughout the summer. Flowers are edible, but most foragers patiently wait for the delectable summer fruits. Roots are most potent spring or fall.

FOOD USE: Snack on fresh fruits. Puree and dry as fruit leather. Make raspberry syrup, jam, vinegar or liqueur. For year-round use, freeze, can, or dehydrate. Dry leaves for tea (see Note below); and combine with fresh or dry raspberries for a flavorsome beverage (serve hot or iced).

HEALTH USE: Fruits are high in vitamins B and C and the minerals magnesium, calcium, iron, and phosphorus, as well as antioxidant flavonoids and ellagic acid (substances documented to be antiviral and anticarcinogenic). Raspberry is a prime ingredient in female reproductive herbal formulas. Leaves contain fragrine, which tones reproductive organs. Raspberry juice and syrup are used to reduce fever in children and adults. Root decoctions relieve diarrhea and dysentery. Leaf infusions are an astringent wash for bleeding gums and mouth sores. Leaf and root poultices are traditionally applied to shingles as well as proud flesh on livestock. In the Middle East, raspberry is widely used to treat kidney stones; a Jordan clinical trial on mice, using raspberry decoctions, confirmed impressive reduction in renal stones as well as a significant preventative effect.

OTHER: Raspberry fruits are a multimillion-dollar industry globally, and pharmaceutical and herbal use continues to escalate. Kim Hummer, in "Rubus Pharmacology: Antiquity to the Present," states, "The consumption of *Rubus* fruits demonstrates a contribution in the prevention of chronic human diseases, improvement of quality of life, and promotion of healthy aging. The pharmacology of *Rubus* presents not only a textbook study of ancient wisdom, but suggests a potential health benefit in humanity's future."

NOTE: In earlier editions of this book, I'd stated that *Rubus* leaves should only be used fresh or thoroughly dried, and that wilted leaves contained cyanide. This supposed "fact" is repeated constantly across the internet. However, after a deep search for a monograph or veterinary research documenting this information, I concur with Mark Williams, teacher of an internet course, *Botany Every Day*, that cyanide is "apparently not present in the Rose subfamily" (to which raspberry belongs.) And even if it were present, any cyanide would be deactivated by heat. If you personally have any doubts regarding raspberry leaf safety, simply abstain from use, or restrict use to fresh or fully dried.

ROSE
Rosa species
Rose family (Rosaceae), Rose subfamily (Rosoideae)

Wild roses perfumed the meadow of my wilderness cabin, triggering deep explorations with its many gifts and resulting in my first published herbal article and new career path. So beware, making rose your herbal ally can be life changing. Wild rose in Alaska has 3 species, all with fragrant 5-petaled pink flowers and many stamens. Leaves are toothed in an odd-pinnate arrangement. After petals drop, the ovary matures into a "rose hip" filled with seeds.

DERIVATION OF NAME: *Rosa* is from the Greek *rhodon*, meaning "red."

OTHER NAMES: wild rose, prickly rose (*R. acicularis*); Nootka rose (*R. nutkana*), wood rose (*R. Woodsii*). Nootka rose is the only one with stems that are mostly unarmed (they may bear some flat prickles). Prickly rose is aptly named.

RANGE: Southeast and Southcentral Alaska to the Brooks Range.

HARVESTING DIRECTIONS: Pick roses in bud or flower stage. Hips are prime after frost.

FOOD USE: Petals are tastiest if you snip and discard the bitter white base. Sprinkle petals on salads. Try a cold-water overnight soak of chopped rose petals (1 tablespoon per cup) for a cool vitamin C–laden refresher. Add petals to cream cheese or dairy-free spreads for crackers. Use in sandwich fillings and omelets. Decorate a cake with the blossoms. Gather hips for free after frost, dry halved or whole; simply strain well after brewing to remove any seedy hairs. In *Botany for a Day*, Thomas Elpel describes the tea as one of his all-time favorites, "even better left in the kettle overnight." Recipes abound on the Internet for making rose hip jelly, jam, syrup, soup, wine, and even vodka. Add rose hip flesh (seeds discarded) to breads, or candied and added to fruitcakes. Rose hip pie is my Thanksgiving treat. Find your favorite pumpkin pie recipe and substitute rose hip puree for the canned pumpkin. To prepare, you can cut each hip in half and scoop out and discard seeds, or do like R.W. Tyler taught me: pinch the hips to expel seeds, retaining the outer flesh. For fastest processing, simmer whole hips in water and process through a food mill (aka mouli); turning the handle pushes the pulp through the fine sieve, and removes the hairy seeds.

HEALTH USE: Hips are high in vitamins A, B, C, E, and K and the minerals calcium and iron. Moistened rose petals are a natural bandage for minor wounds. In a clinical trial, rose hip powder was shown to reduce osteoarthritis symptoms, with over 64% of those studied reporting reduced pain and improved hip flexion." No adverse side effects resulted from rose hip treatment. In another trial, it was demonstrated that rose oil had pain-relieving and antidepressant activities, promoted "physiological and psychological relaxation and had anti-anxiety effects." The *International Journal of Molecular Science* is evaluating numerous rose species as treatments for "skin disorders, hepatotoxicity, renal disturbances, diarrhea, inflammatory disorders, arthritis, diabetes, hyperlipidaemia, obesity and cancer."

OTHER: Rose petals, used as a single ingredient or in combination with elderflowers, are my favorite moisturizing lotion, superb for delicate eye areas, stretch marks, and irritated skin. Discover the delights of making rose beads from the pink portion only of the petals; inhale the soothing fragrance as you macerate thoroughly in a mortar and pestle and shape into beads and dry. Use in jewelry or construct a rosary or mala beads; the beads emit scent when handled during praying or chanting.

CAUTION: The hairs that surround the seeds in rose hips can irritate intestinal linings and cause an "itchy bottom" condition. To avoid irritation, strain rose hip tea with a fine filter.

SHOOTING STAR
Dodecatheon species
Primrose family (Primulaceae)

Shooting stars and beach lovage are 2 native plants I cultivated in my Homer garden for a ready source of salad ingredients. I first discovered shooting stars perched atop rocks by the Gulf of Alaska. I later discovered them growing in great abundance in Yakutat in a meadow, their far more typical habitat. Shooting stars have exquisite bright-pink flowers; the petals bend back, and the long stamens are said to look like a bird's beak (some liken them to a mosquito bill). The basal leaves are light green and taper at the base. The flower stem grows to about 1 foot.

DERIVATION OF NAME: *Dodecatheon* comes from the Greek *dodeka* and *theoi* and means "twelve gods."

OTHER NAMES: frigid shooting star (*D. frigidum*), *dall xilga* (Haida, "rain leaves").

RANGE: Southeast Alaska to the Brooks Range, in habitats ranging from wet or saline meadows to heaths.

HARVESTING DIRECTIONS: Collect leaves spring through summer. Be careful not to disturb or uproot plants after blooming as they are storing energy in the roots for the following spring.

FOOD USE: Shooting star leaves are mild tasting; add to salads and toss with your favorite dressing. Add leaves to spring rolls, tacos, stir-fries. Flowers are an attractive edible garnish.

HEALTH USE: To date, I've found no recorded use of shooting star by Alaska Natives. However, in Canada, Okanagan-Colville and Blackfoot Indians use leaf infusions as a gargle for mouth ulcers, and leaf-root teas are used to treat "sore eyes." In research, I've noticed frequent mention of herbs being used by indigenous people for eye washes and drops and assume such frequent need stems from snow blindness, as well as eye injuries, ailments such as pink eye (bacterial or viral conjunctivitis) or cataracts, as well as irritation from smoky cooking fires.

OTHER: To cultivate shooting star, sprinkle seeds thinly on moist sterile soil in a low, well-drained container. Cover seeds lightly with soil and press down. Keep constantly moist. Sprouts generally appear in 3 weeks and continue appearing for the next 2 weeks. An alternate method is sprinkling seeds on the soil in a garden nursery box just before freeze-up and allowing nature to germinate seeds in spring. They bloom in the third season following planting. Gather seed from the wild in late summer or see the Herbal Directory on page 193. Shooting star flowers are buzz pollinated; bees land on the flowers and vibrate their wings in order in release the pollen from the anthers. Some botanists consider shooting star to be *Primula* subg. *Auriculastrum* sect. *Dodecatheon*.

STRAWBERRY
Fragaria species
Rose family (Rosaceae), Rose subfamily (Rosoideae)

Wild strawberry fruits are smaller than cultivated varieties but superior in flavor. White 5-petaled flowers bearing 5 green sepals and yellow anthers are followed by the familiar red fruits, whose seeds are embedded near the surface. Leaflets are dark green above with silky hairs below and number 3 per stalk. Plants send out runners that root at the joint.

DERIVATION OF NAME: *Fragaria* is from the Latin word for "emit a scent."

OTHER NAMES: wood strawberry, mountain strawberry, earth mulberry, wild strawberry. *atsaaʔaq* (Yupik), *shúk* (Tlingit).

RANGE: Southcentral Alaska to Kodiak, in the Aleutian Islands, and along the central and eastern Yukon River.

HARVESTING DIRECTIONS: Pick fruits when red and juicy. Gather young tender leaves in spring and summer. Flowers are also edible, but most people delay gratification for the fruit.

FOOD USE: Nibble on strawberries as you harvest. Add to your morning cereal or smoothie. Make strawberry jam, strawberry syrup, strawberry pies. Layer fruits in parfaits. Blend with Greek yogurt or coconut yogurt. Blend frozen strawberries with frozen bananas for a dairy-free "ice cream." Puree strawberries and dry as fruit leather; or dry halved berries and add to trail muesli. Brew a strawberry wine. The leaves, together with the mashed fruits, are a tasty tea.

HEALTH USE: Fruits are high in vitamins A and C and minerals calcium, potassium, iron, and sulfur. Strawberry fruit-leaf tea is an herbal tonic. Whereas the fruits alone are a gentle laxative, the leaves balance the brew with their mild astringency. *Fragaria* has been a people's remedy for centuries, used by pregnant women for alleviating morning sickness. Today, strawberry's health benefits are being verified by a plethora of clinical trials. The *Journal of Agricultural and Food Chemistry* shows *Fragaria* to have antioxidant, antimicrobial, anti-inflammatory, cardio and neuroprotective, antidiabetic, antiobesity, and anticancer properties.

OTHER: Indulge in a strawberry beauty masque by mashing berries with a bit of honey and massaging onto your face; rinse well after 5 minutes. In the medieval *Hortus Sanitatis*, a recipe for throat ulcers blended strawberries and plantain tea with mulberry juice and vinegar and "a litre of the dung of a white dog." This recipe, thankfully, has fallen out of use.

CAUTION: Allergies to fresh strawberries can occur, especially in those with birch pollen allergies. Allergies can be triggered by the sprays used extensively on commercially grown strawberries, particular strawberry varieties, or strawberries in general.

WILD CHIVE
Allium schoenoprasum
Amaryllis family (Amaryllidaceae, formerly Lily, Liliaceae),
Onion subfamily (Allioideae)

Chives are unusual in that the cultivated and wild species are one and the same. Leaves and flowers are edible, but must be differentiated from death camas, *Toxicoscordion venenosum*, formerly *Zigadenus elegans* (see page 180). Chives have a hollow leaf, lilac-colored flowers, and an onion scent; death camas has flat leaves and white flowers, and all parts of camas lack an onion aroma.

DERIVATION OF NAME: *Allium* is from the Latin for "garlic" or "onion"; *schoenoprasum* means "reed-like."

OTHER NAMES: wild onion, *paatitaaq* (Iñupiaq), *jelch-táche* (Tlingit, "raven odor").

RANGE: Southeast Alaska to the Brooks Range.

HARVESTING DIRECTIONS: Leaves are prime before flowers appear. If trimmed at the base, they may be harvested repeatedly during the green season. Pick flowers at their peak.

FOOD USE: Steep chive flowers in rice vinegar until flowers turn pale; strain and enjoy this striking lilac-colored, onion-scented vinegar in salad dressings and marinades. Add fresh or dried chopped chives to dips, spreads, soups, egg dishes, potato dishes, herbal butters, or sour-cream toppings. Chives are my favored addition to my dairy-free cashew cheese spread. To marinate fish, blend chopped chives with olive oil and garlic. Top salads with chive flower petals. Dry or freeze chives for year-round use; or do like the Dena'ina Athabascans and pack chives in rock salt (rinse salted chives before using).

HEALTH USE: Wild chive is both antimicrobial and antifungal. Apply chive tea externally to relieve sunburn pain. For sore throat, gargle with a cup of strained chive tea and ¼ teaspoon salt, or use this solution in a neti pot to ease nasal congestions. Romanian clinical trials document its efficacy in reducing inflammation. An Indonesian clinical trial of *kucai* (chive bulb) tincture demonstrated its ability to lower high blood pressure. An Asian trial demonstrated the efficacy of wild chive oil as a larvicide for malaria carrying mosquitos.

OTHER: Include chives in an Alaska-strength "bug off" oil to repel mosquitoes. Chives are an aphid-repelling companion plant for peas and lettuce. You can also make a chive tea aphid spray with 1 or 2 drops of an eco-friendly dish detergent added.

CAUTION: An excess of chive greens can cause digestive upset. Eat in moderation.

Marshes, Ponds, Creeks & Wetlands

Marshes, ponds, and wetlands are environments in which mare's tail and cattail thrive in standing water, and bog cranberry weaves through spongy carpets of sphagnum moss. This habitat is rich in plants that are "traditional medicinals." Food offerings tend to be more seasonal.

Alaska encompasses over 400 million acres, and of this area, nearly half classifies as wetlands. Wetland technically includes the marshes and swampy pond edges discussed in this section, as well as salt marshes (whose plants like goosetongue are addressed in Sea and Sandy Shores on page 31). Compared to the rest of the United States (excluding Hawaii), Alaska contains 63% of total wetland acreage.

BOG CRANBERRY

Oxycoccus microcarpus, aka *Vaccinium microcarpum*,
Vaccinium oxycoccos (formerly *Oxycoccus microcarpus*)
Heath family (Ericaceae)

Bog cranberry is a plant that requires a hands-and-knees approach and scrutiny of its miniscule thread-like stem that weaves through boggy sphagnum carpet. It bears bright pink shooting star–like flowers and plump, delicious berries that appear out of proportion to the size of the plant. This circumboreal species has a long tradition of use.

DERIVATION OF NAME: *Oxycoccus* is Greek for "acid berry."

OTHER NAMES: moss cranberry, swamp cranberry, *tumaglziq* (Yupik), *dah* (Haida).

RANGE: Southeast Alaska to the Alaska Peninsula and north to the Brooks Range, with sporadic occurrences in the Aleutians and the northernmost Arctic.

HARVESTING DIRECTIONS: Pick the berries in late summer; they are sweeter after frost. You can also pick overwintered fruits in spring, though they're generally sparse and may taste slightly fermented (spring fruits are reputed to make birds a tad tipsy).

FOOD USE: Bog cranberries are tasty raw or cooked. Add to pancakes and nut breads, or grind with lingonberries, deseeded rose hips, and citrus for a Thanksgiving relish. Process into jams and jellies. Prepare as juice or herbal liqueur. Dry fruits and grind; add 1 teaspoon of the powder to smoothies.

HEALTH USE: In *Plants That We Eat*, Anore Jones details how Iñupiat elders of Northwest Alaska drank bog cranberry tea for bladder infection and applied mashed berry poultice for easing sore throat and waist rash (like shingles). "To increase the appetite," states Jones, "cranberries were mixed with seal or fish oil and eaten." Some individuals list bog cranberry as a "superfruit" due to the high antioxidant value of the berries. Scientific studies by Czech and Slovakian researchers corroborate presence of urinary tract protectant proanthocyanidins in the fruits, as well as antibacterial and antifungal properties (quercetin and anthocyanins). Constituents are also considered cardioprotective with anticancer activities.

OTHER: Folklore recommends rubbing cranberry juice on your skin at night to remove a faded tan, rinsing well each morning and following with a moisturizer. Will this application help fade freckles or age spots? Be the first to find out.

CAUTION: Clean habitat is essential for safe harvest. In Poland, bog cranberry fruits growing in bogs "influenced by exhausts of the former Black Triangle, one of the most heavily industrialized and polluted areas in Europe" demonstrated its ability to accumulate elevated metal levels, including lithium, nickel, manganese, copper, and zinc. See the *Journal of Environmental Science and Health* for additional details.

SWEET GALE
Myrica gale
Wax myrtle family (Myricaceae)

Sweet gale is a woody shrub with fragrant foliage. Leaves are smooth on the sides and toothed at the top, hence their descriptive local Iliamna Dena'ina name, *dlin'a lu,* or "mouse's hand." Crush sweet gale and inhale its sweet perfume. In spring, in areas where the herb is prolific, it can be identified from afar by the golden cast of its pollen-laden male flowers.

DERIVATION OF NAME: *Myrica* is derived from the Greek "to perfume"; *gale* may be derived from the Greek for "leather helmet," as the male catkins appear in stacked leathery looking layers.

OTHER NAMES: bog myrtle, Alaskan bay, *enem tepkegtsuutii* (Yupik).

RANGE: In swampy areas from Southeast to the Alaska Peninsula and through western and interior Alaska.

HARVESTING DIRECTIONS: Pick the fragrant buds from fall through spring. Pick leaves in summer.

FOOD USE: Use a sweet gale leaf in soups as a substitute for bay leaf. My homemade "land and sea-soning" spice blend contained dry ground sweet gale in combination with seaweed and other herbs. Use buds whole or ground to season stews; proceed slowly as flavor can be overpowering. A little goes a long way.

HEALTH USE: Ethnopharmacological uses of *Myrica gale* range from treatment of ulcers and cardiac disorders to sore muscle relief, and to kill intestinal worms as well as external skin parasites. Sweet gale is an old New England remedy for colds and flu. I like the tea blended with cayenne and ginger. Dena'ina Athabascans drink the brew for tuberculosis. Scandinavians used the boiled herb as an external wash for lice and itchy skin ailments. Clinical trials evaluating the antioxidant and anti-inflammatory activities of *Myrica* have demonstrated highest levels of compounds in the leaves, bark, and roots.

OTHER: Use a sweet gale switch in the sauna for stimulating skin circulation. Essential oil of sweet gale scents male aftershaves. My attempt at "sweet gale cologne" for my husband ended up being a hit as a hot toddy base. Sweet gale, yarrow, and Labrador tea are ingredients in the mildly narcotic "gruit" beer, popular since the Middle Ages. According to Steven Buhner in *Sacred and Healing Herbal Beers*, this is a highly intoxicating beer and in sufficient quantity "stimulates the mind, creates euphoria, and enhances sexual drive." Buhner adds that sweet gale was such an important commerce item in Norway that rents for farms could be paid in *Myrica gale.*

CAUTION: Though safe when used in moderation, sweet gale contains an oil that in excess can trigger vomiting and abortion. It is contraindicated during pregnancy.

CATTAIL
Typha latifolia
Cattail family (Typhaceae)

"A hot dog on a stick" is how author Thomas Elpel describes the appearance of cattail flowers in *Botany in a Day*. This distinctive plant likes wet feet, bears sword-like leaves, and has trailing underground rootstalks (rhizomes) and is unmistakable when in flower. The male flowers resemble an "upper hot dog" that falls off after pollens are released; the lower persistent female "hot dog" progresses from green to golden to brown. Cattails bear gifts for foragers in all seasons, but if gathering when non-flowering, be positive of your ability to differentiate from the sword-leaved wild iris (*Iris* species).

DERIVATION OF NAME: *Typha* is the Greek name for "cattail"; *latifolia* means "broad-leaved."

OTHER NAMES: cat-o-nine tails, Cossack asparagus, rushes, flags.

RANGE: Cattail grows primarily in the Interior from Tanana to Big Delta and sporadically in Southcentral Alaska.

HARVESTING DIRECTIONS: Pick the female flower in spring when firm and green. Collect the golden pollen from the upper male flower by placing a paper bag over the flower, bending the stem, and shaking vigorously. Cut out the cattail heart, the starchy ball at the base of the green stem, and the white rootstalk. In fall, dig the rootstalk. Remove the horn-like sprouts for a vegetable. Process the starch-filled rootstalks for a white flour by scrubbing well. Peel the tough outer rind; then pound with a mallet and cover with water in a jar. The flour will settle to the bottom. Pour off the water, discarding stringy fibers. Use the flour immediately, or dry for future use.

FOOD USE: Hungry for corn on the cob, Alaska style? Steam the green female flower briefly and drizzle with butter and a pinch of salt. Substitute cattail pollen or cattail flour for up to half the flour in biscuit and muffin recipes. Stir-fry cattail hearts.

HEALTH USE: For wilderness toothaches, survival teacher Tom Brown advocates rubbing the sticky juice found between young cattail leaves on the gums surrounding the affected tooth to dull the pain. Add female flowers to salves for scratches and cuts. According to clinical trials published in *BMC Complementary and Alternative Medicine*, oxidative stress, associated with inflammatory bowel disease, was reduced in rats whose diets included 10% cattail rhizome flour.

OTHER: For campers, cattail down is a good tinder for fire-starting. Leaves have been used by diverse people for basketry, caning chairs, bedding materials, torches. Globally, cattail has potential as a food source for a hungry planet. *Western Edible Wild Plants* author H.D. Harrington notes that pollen from 1 acre of cattails is estimated to yield about 6,475 pounds of flour containing 80% carbohydrates and 6% to 8% protein. Numerous studies are demonstrating cattail's ability to remove toxic metals ranging from arsenic to lead via phytoremediation. As always, be certain you are harvesting in a clean habitat.

MARE'S TAIL
Hippuris vulgaris
Plantain family (Plantaginaceae, formerly Water milfoil family,
Haloragaceae), Water starwort tribe (Callitricheae)

Though mare's tail and horsetail (see page 64) aren't even remotely related, the two are sometimes confused. Compare the plants: you'll note that mare's tails are soft in texture and lack the gritty silica of horsetail stems. Tug on mare's tail: it lacks the picture-puzzle capabilities of horsetail, whose stems pull apart and fit back together neatly. Even mature mare's tail leaves are less than an inch long (horsetail's jointed leaves keep growing). Mare's tail leaves are arranged in whorls variable with species, from 4 to 12. Mare's tail develops tiny red wind-pollinated flowers at the junction of leaf and stem; horsetail has spore-bearing cone-like heads located at the top of the fertile stems. To be honest, mare's tail is a plant I've personally only used occasionally to supplement camping fare, as I didn't have ready access to it at my cabin. I'm deeply indebted to Ann Fienup-Riordan for sharing Yup'ik knowledge of food use of this plant.

DERIVATION OF NAME: *Hippuris* is from the Greek word for "pony."

OTHER NAMES: goosegrass, *tayarut* (Yup'ik).

RANGE: Throughout Alaska.

HARVESTING DIRECTIONS: Collect the aboveground portion from spring through summer, as well as fall after the ice forms.

FOOD USE: In Yup'ik villages, mare's tail (*tayarut*) is an important green and used in a myriad of ways. It is cooked with goose and duck, boiled with whitefish, caribou, moose, or rabbit, or cooked in broth with salmon roe or burbot eggs. The plants are collected in early spring, as well as during the summer and autumn while still green. Another harvest period is after freeze-up when the plants are wilted. Harvesting methods vary according to season. Sometimes the plants are raked up and substantial qualities are collected. If the marsh is frozen, they may be scraped with a shovel. Brown, wintered-over mare's tail is an early spring vegetable; the herb changes to bright green when cooked. During long winters and famine times, *tayarut* mixed with seal oil was of vital importance to survival.

HEALTH USE: In Siberia, *Hippuris vulgaris* (Alaska's most common mare's tail species) was used by Kacha Native people for curing fever. This plant, referred to as *tudan-ot*, also served as a smudge plant but it's unrecorded whether this was for ceremonial purposes or warding off illness. In Tibetan medicine, a *Hippuris* species is used to heal internal lung damage from weapon injuries.

OTHER: Mare's tail is used as an oxygenating plant in bog gardens and chemical-free pools to inhibit algae (5 plants per 1,000 quarts).

CAUTION: Gather mare's tail in clean areas.

MARSH MARIGOLD
Caltha palustris
Buttercup family (formerly Crowfoot family, Ranunculaceae)

Is marsh marigold poisonous or safe? The answer is both. Marsh marigold contains the compound protoanemonin, a toxic lactone common in the buttercup family. Ingested raw, the plant can trigger symptoms ranging from nausea and dizziness to blistering of the mucosa to spasms and more. Drying or boiling renders the toxin innocuous and makes the plant safe to eat (the toxin dissipates at 180°F). Marsh marigold is easily recognized by its round to kidney-shaped leaves and by its bright yellow flowers, which grow on trailing stems that rise up at the ends. Marsh marigold has green seed-filled capsules. Be sure to read all guidelines thoroughly before harvesting.

DERIVATION OF NAME: *Caltha* is the Latin name for "marigold;" *palustris* means "marsh-loving."

OTHER NAMES: cowslip, meadowbout, palsywort, meadowbright, marybud, horse blob.

RANGE: Throughout Alaska.

HARVESTING DIRECTIONS: Marsh marigold leaves are prime before flowering. They are one of the first spring greens to appear and survive the late frosts. Gather flower buds when tightly closed.

FOOD USE: When I was wilderness camping and hungry for greens to accompany the evening salmon, marsh marigold was present in abundance. I boiled the greens in 2 changes of water, as recommended, with very satisfactory results. I've also pickled flower buds (after blanching) and used as a substitute for capers. Researchers studying *Wild Food Plants Used by the Tibetans of Gongba Valley* noted: "The culinary use of *Caltha palustris* as a green vegetable is very interesting. In its raw state, marsh marigold is a toxic plant, due to the presence of protoanemonin. In this area it is dried or lactofermented before use."

HEALTH USE: *Caltha*'s primary health use is externally as a poultice for insect bites and sore muscles. *Caltha* species have some history of internal low dose, short-term use for loosening mucus in chest and sinuses.

OTHER: Mashed leaves were once used as a treatment for warts. Marsh marigolds are a good addition to backyard bog gardens. They are described as "emergent pond plants" as they root in shallow water but then emerge, growing vertically into the air like land plants.

CAUTION: Use marsh marigold in moderation only. Daily use can cause kidney or liver inflammation. Handling the raw herb can irritate sensitive skin. Be positive of identification, as wild calla (*Calla palustris* on page 181) frequents the same wet habitat.

DOCK & SORREL

Rumex species
Buckwheat family (Polygonaceae)

DOCK (before flowering)

SHEEP SORREL

Dock is the name commonly used for the more robust *Rumex* species, whereas sorrel is typically used for the smaller, more strongly lemon-tasting species. The genus as a whole is highly adaptable, ranging from the extremes of the Arctic to the tropics. Like dandelions and plantain, they are often cursed as a "weed," but for Alaska Natives and rural residents, docks play a major role in food and well-being. Docks have leaves arranged in a basal cluster; the central stalk grows to 4 feet in height and bears an abundance of seeds in papery reddish capsules. *Rumex* species include arrow-leaf-shaped sheep sorrel (*R. acetosella*) as well as narrower-leaved *R. graminifolius* of western coastal Alaska.

DERIVATION OF NAME: Believed to be derived from the classical Latin name *Rumex* for sorrel, or possibly *rumo* ("to suck"), due to the thirst-quenching properties of chewing sorrel.

OTHER NAMES: sourdock, sourgrass, wild spinach; wild rhubarb, curly dock (*R. crispus*); Arctic dock (*R. arcticus*), *quunarlziq* (Yup'ik), *tł'aaqw'ách* (Tlingit, "wild rhubarb"), *tl'aangk'uus* (Haida), *ash'i* (Dena'ina), *quagaq* (Inuit).

RANGE: Throughout Alaska.

HARVESTING DIRECTIONS: Collect leaves for food in spring to summer when bright green in color. Avoid older red leaves. Gather seeds in late summer. Roots are prime in fall or spring.

FOOD USE: Sorrels have a refreshing lemony tang; docks have a hint of lemon and more astringency. Iñupiat blend boiled dock leaves with berries, blubber, and seal oil and ferment it in wooden kegs. In many villages, dock is frozen for winter use. I've added young leaves to casseroles, quiche, salad dressings, and boiled dinners. Sorrels add lemony zest to a salad and salad dressings. In famines, seeds can be ground as a flour extender; they are tedious to collect and process.

HEALTH USE: Clinical trials of *Rumex crispus* document that it is protective against osteoporosis as it prevents microstructural deterioration. Diverse species are demonstrated to be cytoprotective antioxidants, with anti-inflammatory, analgesic, and cytotoxic properties. Another trial on western dock, published in the *International Journal of Dermatology*, concluded that *Rumex* 3% cream "is comparable in efficacy with 4% hydroquinone cream" as a skin-lightening agent for melasma (a hyperpigmentation on face, neck and arms). Throughout the ages, dock has been used by people of diverse cultures for skin problems, anemia, hepatitis, liver damage, and cleansing the system of heavy metals. Wilderness campers can mash dock root as a poultice for relief of bee stings, blisters, or boils. Yup'ik Natives drink dock-leaf juice for colds and upset stomach.

CAUTION: Docks and sorrel, as well as beet greens, spinach, lettuce, lamb's quarter, etc. naturally contain the salt oxalic acid. Oxalic acid is also present, in high concentrations in manufactured bleaches and metal cleaners. The oxalic acid poisonings reported in the literature most often involve grazing animals or industrial products. People have been safely eating docks and other greens containing oxalic acid for centuries. What is important is that you have a varied and balanced diet. Note that cooking wilting or fermenting greens reduces their oxalic acid content. Those who *do* need to be especially careful regarding oxalic acid intake include individuals with gout, kidney disorders, or rheumatoid arthritis. If in doubt, consult your doctor.

JEWELWEED
Impatiens noli-tangere
Touch-me-not family (Balsaminaceae)

My relationship with jewelweed dates back to childhood. I delighted in touching the mature seeds and marveling as they shot forth like a cannon, with the seed casing dramatically coiling like a spent rubber band. Even as an elder, I'm equally enchanted with the "game," but my appreciation for *Impatiens* today extends to the bountiful gifts of this globetrotting jewel. Jewelweed thrives in moist shady areas. The slipper-shaped yellow flowers taper to a narrow end with a curved spur. Coarsely toothed leaves alternate along the smooth stems and have a water-repellent coating. For a "magic trick," submerge the leaves in water; watch their undersides turn silvery, like a shimmering jewel. The stem is hollow, and very juicy when rubbed firmly.

DERIVATION OF NAME: *Impatiens* means "impatient;" *noli-tangere* translates as "no-touch." Both refer to explosive mature seedpods.

OTHER NAMES: touch-me-not, slipperweed, snapweed, quick-in-the-hand.

RANGE: Southeast and Southcentral Alaska, and sporadically through western Alaska and the Interior. Globally, jewelweed ranges from North America to Eurasia.

HARVESTING DIRECTIONS: Pick young shoots and leaves when under 1 foot tall. Gather flowers from tall summer stalks. Collect seeds when pods spring at the touch.

FOOD USE: Young greens are suitable as a vegetable, provided they are cooked. Boil in 2 changes of water for 10 minutes each time; strain, save and freeze the first water in ice cubes for health use. Add the flowers to stir-fries. Collect unhusked seeds by placing a bag over mature seed heads, bend stems carefully, and bump the plant gently. Use for a nutty flavor in breads and muffins.

HEALTH USE: Apply crushed jewelweed as a poultice on skin ailments ranging from mosquito bites and nettle stings to poison ivy and cow parsnip burns. Or soothe inflamed skin with your jewelweed juice "ice cubes." A Romanian clinical study of jewelweed, published in *ScienceDirect* concludes: "The results of this study confirm the folklore use of *I. noli-tangere…* extracts as a natural anti-inflammatory agent and justify its ethnobotanical use." Greens are also a common ingredient in salves for athlete's foot, warts, and ringworm.

OTHER: Seeds are good feed for wild or caged birds. In 1672, in New England, writer John Josselyn touted jewelweed ointment as a "sovereign remedy for bruises of what kind so ever."

CAUTION: Jewelweed contains plant-protective biominerals that in excess can contribute to kidney-stone formation. Boiling the plant in changes of water significantly reduces the soluble oxalate content.

MONKEYFLOWER

Erythranthe guttata (formerly *Mimulus guttatus*)
Lopseed family (Phrymaceae,
formerly Figwort family, Scrophulariaceae)

I always feel happy when I see monkeyflowers. They're a worldwide companion, greeting me with their cheer-me-up blooms from Alaska's wilds to my present New Zealand neighborhood. The bright yellow blossoms have a tube-like structure, irregular petals with a long lower lip, and red spots inside the flower. Leaves have irregular teeth. Leaves are opposite, with the lower leaves having a short stalk, whereas the upper are sessile (lacking a stalk).

DERIVATION OF NAME: *Erythranthe* is from the Greek *erythros* and *anthos*, meaning "red flower" (monkeyflowers are yellow!). It was formerly *Mimulus guttatus*, which translates to "speckled mimic" (said to look like a spotted monkey's face).

OTHER NAMES: yellow monkeyflower, common monkeyflower.

RANGE: Southeast and Southcentral Alaska to the Aleutian Islands and north to the Yukon River.

HARVESTING DIRECTIONS: Though monkeyflower greens are often collected before flowering, they remain palatable throughout the summer season. Pick blossoms at their peak. Greens can sometimes be found in winter, under the ice.

FOOD USE: For a Greek salad, toss monkeyflower greens, spring beauty, saxifrage, and other available wild edibles together and top with feta cheese and olives. Garnish with monkeyflower blossoms and add a splash of dressing. Add the blooms to homemade gelatin salads and floral salads.

HEALTH USE: Mash stems and flowers as a poultice for insect bites, minor cuts and scratches, and rope burns. Apply stems and leaves in steambaths for backache and sore chests. Decoctions were traditionally drunk to relieve stomach upset. Alutiiq in the Chugach region drank monkeyflower infusions and decoctions to relieve constipation.

OTHER: Monkeyflower greens were steamed by early American settlers as a potherb, a use equally applicable today. *Mimulus* was one of the first 12 Bach floral essences, recommended for shy, nervous people with multiple known fears. A scientific study on monkeyflower by Roels and Kelly demonstrated its ability to evolve rapidly and become self-pollinating after losing access to its traditional bee pollinators.

AMERICAN VERONICA

Veronica americana

Plantain family (Plantaginaceae, formerly Figwort family, Scrophulariaceae), Speedwell tribe (Veroniceae)

Veronica is one of the many plants that has been botanically reclassified, shunted from the figwort family into the plantain family with its own new subfamily. Present methods of classifying this family are based on nuclear ribosomal analysis rather than its classic "family pattern" characteristics. Despite this botanical mishmash of confusion, veronica is an easy plant to get to know. At first glance, veronica is a rather inconspicuous herb. But look more closely at roadside ditches and wet places. The dainty blue flowers somewhat resemble Alaska's state flower, the forget-me-not. But veronica's flowers have 4 unequal petals and 2 prominent stamens. Its seed purses are heart-shaped, and its leaves are gently toothed and arranged in pairs. Stems are rounded.

DERIVATION OF NAME: *Veronica* is named after Saint Veronica who wiped Christ's face on way to the Crucifixion and was left with Christ's "true face" (*Vera iconica*) on her cloth. *Americana* means "American."

OTHER NAMES: speedwell, American brooklime.

RANGE: Southeast Alaska to the northern Alaska Peninsula, easterly to the Yukon River, and throughout the Aleutian Islands.

HARVESTING DIRECTIONS: Harvest these water-loving greens in clean areas; some foragers wash the greens in water with a water-purifier tablet added. Leaves are prime before flowering; I continue to gather the flowering tops throughout the summer season.

FOOD USE: Japanese, East Asians, and Europeans consider veronica a delicacy and compare it to watercress in flavor. The vitamin C–rich spring greens can form the bulk of a salad. Add chopped greens to egg salad and potato salads. Include in veggie or fish burgers. Summer greens can be blanched or marinated to tame the flavor.

HEALTH USE: In old herbals, veronica was classed as an expectorant to help clear lungs of mucus and used as tea or syrup for easing bronchitis, asthma, and coughs. Clinical studies by Austrian researches, published in the *Journal of Ethnopharmacology*, verify veronica's effects on the respiratory tract, nervous and cardiovascular systems, and metabolism.

OTHER: *Veronica* is said to honor the saint who wiped Christ's face on the way to the crucifixion. According to legend, a shepherd whose king was gravely ill observed an injured deer heal its wound by eating and rolling in veronica. The shepherd reported the sighting; the king regained his health with veronica and showered wealth on the shepherd. Though your acquaintance with veronica may not bring riches, its use can save coins in the household.

SPRING BEAUTY

Claytonia species

Miner's Lettuce family (Montiaceae, formerly Purslane, Portulacaceae)

One of my favorite creekside plants is the dainty Siberian spring beauty, *Claytonia sibirica*. This attractive annual grew in profusion along stream edges and in moist, shady places en route to my wilderness cabin. Flowers have 5 pink or white petals. Leaves are on single stems in a basal cluster, and in pairs on the flowering stems. The greens remain mild flavored throughout the growing season. Due to genetic analysis by botanists, the *Claytonias* have now been shifted from the purslane family to the miner's lettuce family.

DERIVATION OF NAME: Claytonia honors 17th-century botanist John Clayton.

OTHER NAMES: Siberian spring beauty, Siberian miner's lettuce, *tł'aangq'uus xil* (Haida).

RANGE: Southeast and Southcentral Alaska to the Aleutian Islands and the Arctic.

HARVESTING DIRECTIONS: Though some guides advocate eating the entire green portion, I prefer to selectively pinch off leaves and blossoms. Make certain to leave an abundance of flowers to set seed and propagate the species.

FOOD USE: All of Alaska's 11 *Claytonia* species have edible leaves and flowers and are a great trail nibble. Add to salads and vegetable dishes. Some species like *C. tuberosa* and *C. acutifolia* have edible corms and taproots traditionally eaten by Native people. They are reported to have a "chestnut-like" flavor. Indiscriminate harvesting by foragers has endangered these plants in some regions.

HEALTH USE: Leaves are high in vitamins A and C. *Native American Ethnobotany* records use of mashed plant as poultice for wounds and rheumatic joints; leaf juice is traditional medicine for sore eyes and snowblindness. Tlingit applied a salve of spring beauty, spruce pitch, and Alaskan cypress bark (*Chamaecyparis nootkatensis*) externally for treating venereal disease.

OTHER: The annual *Claytonia sibirica* grows well in garden soil and self-seeds freely. The perennial *C. sarmentosa* has fewer flowers and produces bud-bearing runners. *C. perfoliata*, commonly called miner's lettuce, is known to occur in Unalaska; this species has distinctive round leaves through which stems and flowers emerge.

MOUNTAIN SORREL
Oxyria digyna
Buckwheat family (Polygonaceae)

"The pause that refreshes" is a commercial slogan that could easily apply to mountain sorrel. When hiking the long switchback to my wilderness cabin, I always enjoyed pausing at Wolverine Creek and nibbling the tart, lemon-fresh leaves growing in the sunny rocky edges. Mountain sorrel is low to the ground, with a compact basal cluster of distinctive leaves. Leaves are round to kidney-shaped and each borne on a single stem. The flowering stems grow 6 to 12 inches high and bear reddish-green flowers followed by clusters of flat seeds.

DERIVATION OF NAME: *Oxyria* refers to the sharp, pungent taste of the leaf; *digyna* refers to its 2 floral carpels.

OTHER NAMES: sourgrass, alpine mountain sorrel, *kitłuq* (Iñupiaq), *kungluk* (Yup'ik).

RANGE: Throughout Alaska in wet places, and snow beds in mountains and tundra.

HARVESTING DIRECTIONS: Gather sorrel leaves in spring and summer. The green leaves are much preferred to the later season red leaves.

FOOD USE: The tart lemony leaves of sorrel are a thirst-quencher on camping trips. Add leaves to salads, salad dressings, sandwiches, and campfire creations. Sorrel's tangy flavor blends especially well with fish. Make a creamy French style *soupe à l'oseille* (sorrel soup), with a big bunch of chopped sorrel, diced onion and potatoes, seasonings, and fresh cream. Blend sorrel with butter for a delicious spread. Simmer leaves in water to make a sweet "lemonade" (add honey or sugar if desired). In the Arctic, mountain sorrel is eaten fresh or preserved in seal oil. It is reported to be one of the "tundra greens" most eaten by Baffin Island Inuit. Add sorrel with cabbage for fermented sauerkraut.

HEALTH USE: Leaves are a good source of vitamin C. Mountain sorrel is eaten after meals to aid digestion. Nunavut Inuit use mountain sorrel infusions to ease stomach aches caused by too much fat intake. Mashed sorrel leaves have been used as a poultice for warts and skin irritations.

OTHER: Flavor of mountain sorrel is very similar to that of the arrow-leaved dock species and the cultivated garden sorrel (*R. acetosa*). All can be used interchangeably. Both *Oxyria* and *Rumex* are in the buckwheat family. Both wild and cultivated sorrels are easy to grow in northern gardens. The closely related *Rumex acetosa* is the base of a famous French *soupe aux herbes*.

CAUTION: Consume sorrel in moderation only. See Caution for dock on page 163 for oxalic acid details.

Poisonous Plants

Poisonous plants are common in gardens as they are often dramatically showy. Fruits like red baneberries look spray-painted; white baneberries look like doll's eyes. Leaves may have dramatic appearance (like false hellebore, as seen here).

Following is a listing of toxic plants, primarily those that could be confused with other plants in this book. Other poisonous plants also occur in Alaska. Before consuming any plant, be positive of identification. Consult medical help immediately if you experience any adverse reaction.

POISON HEMLOCK aka WATER HEMLOCK
Cicuta mackenzieana, C. douglasii
Parsley family (Apiaceae, formerly Umbelliferae)

Of all the plants in Alaska, the poison/water hemlocks demand the most respect. *Cicuta* is, by far, the state's most toxic plant. Even a leaf nibble has hospitalized foragers, and 1 to 3 bites of root has triggered renal failure, seizures, delirium, ventricular fibrillations, and death. A child using a *Cicuta* stem as a whistle also died. Years ago, while merely holding the stem of an uprooted hemlock to show details to students, my hand and arm began tingling like I was touching an electric fence. I'm now aware that absorption of cicutoxin is rapid and occurs through the skin as well as through the gut.

Cicuta mackenzieana, Alaska's predominant species, ranges from the Kenai Peninsula to Kodiak to the Alaska Peninsula and north to the Brook's Range. It has long narrow leaves, which some foragers mistake for marijuana (*Cannabis*). The broader-leafed *Cicuta douglasii* ranges from Southeast and south coastal Alaska to Kodiak and the Kenai Peninsula.

Like all parsley/celery plant family members, poison hemlock bears compound umbels. Flower stems radiate from a single point, like the spokes of an umbrella, and from the top of each "spoke" is a second set of umbels. Learn this family pattern as it is key to this family of both delightful, as well as deadly, plants. Many books describe *Cicuta's* roots as "chambered." That is, if sliced open, they resemble a potato with slits cut through it, and bits of the potato between the slits scooped out to form chambered compartments. But you shouldn't be handling the root, due to gut absorption of cicutoxin. And root chambering is not a reliable identification method. (I've found *Cicuta* roots heaved above the ground

176

surface by frost that were not chambered, similar to a solid potato. Also, healthful plants like *Angelica* are described in floras as having septate (divided into compartments) roots.

An identifier I find more reliable (in combination with marshy habitat and umbel shape) is the pattern of leaf veins. Examine with a loupe (magnifier) and you will notice that *Cicuta*'s main leaf veins end at the bottom of the V between the toothed leaf margins, whereas the primary veins of lovage and angelica end at the tip of the teeth. The memory-jogging ditty taught me by Robyn Klein of Bozeman, Montana, is: "Vein to the cut, pain in the gut. Vein to the tip, pretty hip."

Cicuta mackenzieana

Cicuta douglasii

FLOWER STAGE

FRUIT STAGE

BANEBERRY aka DOLL'S EYE
Actaea rubra
Buttercup family (formerly Crowfoot family, Ranunculaceae)

A deadly toxic berry! Baneberry is a perennial, averaging 1½ to 3½ feet in height, with toothed compound leaves and clusters of shiny red or white berries with a distinctive black dot at the end. Fruits are extremely bitter. Ingestion can cause sharp pains, mental confusion, bloody diarrhea, and even death due to cardiac arrest or respiratory paralysis. Seek prompt medical attention if ingested.

MONKSHOOD aka WOLFBANE
*Aconitum delphinifolium,
A. maximum*
Buttercup family (formerly Crowfoot family, Ranunculaceae)

Monkshood contains highly poisonous aconitin, a neurotoxic and cardiotoxic alkaloid. Leaves are palmate and could be confused with those of wild geranium (unless the plants are in flower). *Aconitum* blossoms are deep purple (sometimes white) and, as the name indicates, shaped like a monk's hood. Ayurvedic and traditional Chinese medicine practitioners are known to include *Aconitum* in complex formulas; dosage is absolutely critical as the toxins rival those of poison water hemlock (*Cicuta*).

DELPHINIUM aka LARKSPUR

Delphinium species
Buttercup family (formerly
Crowfoot family, Ranunculaceae)

Delphiniums range wildly and widely across mainland Alaska and are also common garden flowers. Like monkshood, all parts of the plant contain cardiotoxic alkaloids. Though historically used externally in treatment of lice, toxins could be absorbed through broken or irritated skin.

FALSE HELLEBORE

Veratrum species
Bunchflower family
(Melanthiaceae, formerly Lily
family, Liliaceae)

Hellebore often grows in similar habitat with edible twisted stalk. Hellebore stems are stouter and bear parallel-veined leaves with deep pleats. Even a nibble can cause constriction in the throat and breathing difficulty. Mature hellebore has a central, tall flowering stalk bearing drooping clusters of greenish flowers. Flowers have 6 tepals (3 petals and 3 sepals of similar size and color). All parts of the plants contain steroidal alkaloids that can cause birth deformities in grazing animals and potential death to human foragers. In early spring, when just emerging from the earth, some foragers have mistaken small hellebore shoots for newly emerging twisted stalk shoots.

FLOWER STAGE

SHOOTS STAGE

POISONOUS PLANTS

DEATH CAMAS

Toxicoscordion venenosum
(formerly *Zigadenus* aka
Zygadenus elegans)
Bunchflower family
(Melanthiaceae,
formerly Lily, Liliaceae)

If you think you've found a wild onion, look again. Unlike the hollow round scented leaves of edible chive, toxic death camas has long flat leaves. Smell the plant. Death camas leaves and bulbs lack an onion scent. All parts of death camas contain zygadenine, an alkaloid that can cause salivation, muscular weakness, impaired breathing, and coma. Death camas thrives in open woods and grassy places and is toxic to both humans and livestock.

ARROWGRASS

Triglochin species
Arrowgrass family
(Juncaginaceae)

Arrowgrass contains a cyanide compound. Symptoms of over-ingestion (typically by grazing animals) include trembling, vomiting, convulsions, and potentially death by asphyxiation. Toxicity increases in spring and when the plant is stressed by drought or lack of frost.

Flowering stems of seaside species (*T. maritima*) can reach 2½ feet. Flowers are in dense spikes. In early spring, foragers are known to confuse the young leaves of arrowgrass with the highly edible goosetongue (*Plantago maritima*). However, don't panic if you accidentally nibble a leaf. The taste is significantly different from salty goosetongue. The toxic dose of cyanide in arrowgrass is not cumulative, and a significant quantity must be eaten at one time. Some guides insist that white leaf bases of arrowgrass are safe to eat, but I prefer to list the entire plant in the toxic class.

BOG ROSEMARY
Andromeda polifolia
Heath family (Ericaceae),
Blueberry subfamily
(Vaccinioideae), Andromeda
tribe (Andromedeae)

Leaves are long and pointed, somewhat resembling Labrador tea. Bog rosemary leaves are pale underneath (they lack Labrador tea's brownish felty undersides). Bog rosemary also lacks a distinct scent when crushed. Flowers are pink bells. The plant contains andromedotoxin, which causes breathing difficulties, cramps, coordination loss, low blood pressure, vomiting, and diarrhea.

WILD CALLA aka BOG ARUM
Calla palustris
Arum family (Araceae)

Calla leaves are similar to those of marsh marigold but come to an abrupt point. The plant bears a central flower spike (spadix) backed by a white modified leaf (spathe). Flowers are followed by clusters of red berries. The plant contains calcium oxalate, which causes intense burning of the mouth and throat. It's said that the burning crystals can be neutralized by thorough drying or boiling, but until more data is available, I regard calla as a toxic plant.

HERBAL PREPARATIONS

Throughout this book, herbal teas (infusions and decoctions), oils, salves, ointments, poultices, and tinctures have been mentioned. An entire book could be written on this topic, but for those new to using herbs as healthful preparations, some basic techniques are addressed here.

Herbal Teas

Herbal tea (or herbal tisane) is the common name for the commercial beverage typically made by steeping a teabag in hot water for 5 minutes. Herbal infusions and decoctions (and medicinal herbal teas) also use water as medium for extracting flavor and constituents. What's different is their purpose, potency, steeping methods, and extraction time. The shelf life of an herbal tea averages 24 to 72 hours.

A general rule of thumb for tonic herbs: Use 1 to 2 tablespoons fresh plant or 1 to 2 teaspoons dry plant per cup water. Your particular choice of plant may require higher or lower quantity.

Cold infusions are different from just chilling a formerly hot tea, though many people are familiar with that concept from iced tea. A cold infusion is actually brewed with cold (or cool) water. It requires a steeping time of 6 to 8 hours. For ease, I generally just steep my herb of choice in cool water overnight in a quart canning jar. Make certain to chop the herb well to maximize extraction, cover with non-chlorinated water, cap, and leave in a cool place. This is an excellent method for:
- herbs high in vitamin C (rose hips, spruce tips).
- aromatic herbs (mint, wild chamomile, spruce tips). This method yields a beverage tea with maximum flavor and aroma as it extracts the light volatile oils.
- plants with delicate flavors (salmonberry flowers).
- plants with mucilage (fireweed, chickweed). Cold extracts the most mucilage for soothing irritated conditions.
- plants with high tannins that you wish to inhibit to avoid stomach upset (uva ursi).

Note: Cold infusions should not be used by those with an impaired immune system, such as those with HIV.

Hot infusions are the hot beverages most people are highly familiar with. The difference between a typical commercial herbal tea and hot infusions for more healthful purposes has to do with the herb chosen, the amount of herbal matter used, and the length of steeping. Generally, an herbal tea for deeper physiological effect is steeped 20 minutes or more. Aromatic plants, when steeped in hot water, release more of their denser steam-released antimicrobial oil. Use a sealed container to prevent the volatile oils from escaping.

Decoctions are made by simmering the plant, covered, for an average of 20 minutes. Begin by placing your chopped plant in a pot, adding cold water, and bringing to a low simmer. Decoctions are used with most roots, inner bark, seeds, and dense plant parts.

Solar infusions, or sun teas, are actually one type of hot infusion. Even if begun with cool water, if left on a sunny windowsill, the sun tea heats to such a degree that it extracts constituents more similar to traditional hot infusions.

Moon infusions, or moon teas, are less well known. Place your herbs and cool water in a canning jar and allow it to sit outdoors in the moonlight. Strain and drink first thing in the morning. These can be highly refreshing and invigorating. Nettle-mint moon tea is one of my favorites.

Herbal Oils, Salves & Ointments

Making your own herbal massage and body oils and soothing salves is an empowering experience.

Use freshly dried herbs to avoid adding excess moisture to your oil. Choose herbs based on your intended purpose for your oil. A single herb may be used, or a combination. For example, cottonwood bud used solo creates an exquisitely fragrant and effective sore muscle and skin soothing oil.

Chop your herbs of choice finely to maximize extraction. Use minimum ⅓ cup herbs per quart oil.

Choose a high-quality oil with a mild scent such as extra-virgin olive, organic canola, almond oil, avocado oil, hemp oil etc. Grapeseed is often used in villages due to its availability at moderate cost. Use the highest quality oil you can afford.

HERBAL OILS
There are a few methods to make oils:

Double Boiler: Place herbs and oil in the top of a double boiler over very low heat until a "color extraction" has taken place (generally 4 to 6 hours).

Crockpot Method 1: Some foragers set the herbs and oil directly in a crockpot or slow cooker. In my experience with my equipment, even when set on the lowest setting, herbs often have a burnt smell.

Crockpot Method 2 (preferred): More reliable is to place the herbs and oil in a glass jar with a lid and immerse the jar in a crockpot filled with hot water. Keep on low for 24 to 72 hours.

Sun-infused: This is a method preferred by some herbalists. Place herbs and oil in a jar in a sunny windowsill, shaking daily, for a 3-week period. Note that if using fresh herbs, mold may occur. It is more reliable to use freshly dried herbs for sun-infused oils.

Whichever method you choose, when the extraction period is complete, strain through clean cotton cloth or multilayers of cheesecloth. Discard herbs. The herbal oil can be used as a massage or moisturizing oil. If you wish, keep part of your product as herbal oil and process part for a salve.

SALVES AND OINTMENTS

To turn oil into a salve or ointment, add beeswax (vegans can use carnauba wax). For 4 tablespoons oil, use 1 tablespoon beeswax; or for 8 ounces of herbal oil, use 2 ounces beeswax.

Place your oil and beeswax in the top of a double boiler (with water gently simmering in lower pot). When the beeswax is melted, test your consistency. Simply dip a teaspoon in the oil/beeswax and set the spoon in the refrigerator to cool. Some folks like a thick salve, and others a thinner one, so if your salve is too hard, add more oil and reheat; if too soft, add more beeswax. When you have your desired consistency, remove from heat. Add essential oils of choice before your beeswax has a chance to set.

For sore muscle oils and ointments, adding essential oils of peppermint or camphor (menthol) is a good choice. They stimulate the nerves and create a warm sensation; enhance with cinnamon or clove for lasting heat. Spruce, birch, lavender, or rosemary are also great. Popular essential oils for skin salves include tea tree, cedar, (antifungal); eucalyptus, thyme (antiseptic), peppermint (for itchy skin, and to increase circulation), lavender (for burns), clove (for pain). For moisturizing ointments use rose, lavender, rosemary, or orange. For insect repellant preparations use pennyroyal, lemon, rosemary, citronella, garlic, or wormwood.

Essential oils are highly concentrated; thus, add a few drops at a time and adjust as desired. On average, you will need 10 to 20 drops per 8 ounces of herbal oil or ointment. Use vitamin E as a preservative: 500 IU per 8-ounce bottle. Be certain to store you oils and ointments in a cool, dark place. Label and date your product.

Herbal Poultices

Poultices are a topical herbal application, typically used to reduce swellings and inflammation, soothe abrasions, and relieve congestion or infection. The herb may be raw or heated. Mash and apply directly to the body or encase in a clean dressing before placing on the skin. Dry powdered plant is sometimes used. If on the trail, just chew the herb and apply to your insect bite or sting and hold in place with a bandage from your first-aid kit.

Some common Alaskan poultices include:

Chickweed: Apply mashed chickweed paste to relieve itchy skin problems or inflammation.

Devil's club: Apply finely chopped and ground stem inner bark (cambium) to a wasp string or to relieve infection from a devil's club prickle.

Elderflower: Mash flowers and apply as a poultice for mild burns or irritated skin.

Fireweed: Mash fresh root or use dry root powder on ulcerated sores.

Horsetail: I've used horsetail poultices effectively for a cyst, as well as infected livestock wounds. Simmer chopped horsetail for 15 minutes and mash with mortar and pestle. Wrap in cloth and secure to the affected area. Apply a fresh dressing 2 to 3 times daily.

Mustard: Apply mustard poultices on the chest for bronchitis, congestion, and chest pain.

Plantain: Plantain is a star for infected wounds. Steep leaves in boiled water. Reserve the largest leaf. Mash the remainder to a pulp, and apply the poultice with the large leaf on top as a bandage.

Wormwood: This is my favorite for sore muscles. Boil chopped wormwood, wrap in a clean cloth, and apply these hot packs to the sore area.

Yarrow: Mash leaves and apply on cuts or insert into the nostril to halt a nosebleed. (This even relieved my horse's nosebleed in minutes.) In my experience, cultivated garden yarrows do not work nearly as well as the wild species.

Tinctures

Tinctures are concentrated plant extracts that use alcohol, vinegar, or glycerin to extract herbal constituents. Advantages include a more potent product, longer shelf life, and portability. Tinctures are great for wilderness first aid kits and air travel. Since a tincture dose is greatly reduced (compared to a tea), they are a great way to take a very strong-tasting herb (for example, highbush cranberry or crampbark).

There are 3 basic choices of menstruum (solvent) for making tinctures. Which solvent to use depends on the herb chosen and your state of health. If you are an alcoholic or living in a "dry" Alaskan village, then definitely choose vegetable glycerin or vinegar.

- Alcohol, as in brandy, vodka, whisky, or other 80-proof drinking alcohol, is most often used for tinctures as it extracts a broad variety of constituents. Alcohol tinctures have the longest shelf life, generally 2 to 5 years.

- Vegetable glycerin, aka glycerin, is a sweet, syrupy liquid typically made from coconut or vegetable oils (tinctures made with glycerin are often referred to as glycerites). Vegetable glycerin works extremely well with aromatic herbs. A mint glycerite, for example, has far superior flavor to a mint alcohol tincture. Take a dropperful to help ease a queasy stomach. A dropper of pineapple weed or wild chamomile glycerite, taken straight or in a little hot water, can facilitate relaxation and sleep. It's also well suited for cranky children.

- Vinegar tinctures are often called vinegar extracts. Vinegar works well for plants with easily extracted constituents. I like a "spring tonic" apple cider vinegar extract for nettles, lovage, chickweed, chive flowers, and leaves. I use this blend in herbal vinaigrettes or added to tea with honey.

If beginning with tincture making, rely on the traditional "Simpler's Method" practiced through the ages, as follows.

Chop your herb of choice finely, pack loosely into a jar, and cover fully with your solvent of choice.

- If alcohol, use undiluted 80-proof (40% alcohol) brandy or vodka.
- If vegetable glycerin, dilute the glycerin. Use 60% vegetable glycerin plus 40% water. Thus, if making a pint of tincture, you would use approximately 10 ounces vegetable glycerin and 6 ounces water).
- If vinegar, use undiluted vinegar, the highest quality you can afford, such as organic apple cider vinegar.

Steep your tincture for 2 to 3 weeks, shaking daily. Then strain, discarding the herb. Store your tincture in dark, well labeled-bottles.

Tincture making can be a highly refined process, as practiced by clinical herbalists and pharmacists. Specific ratios are used for each plant, with lower alcohol used for highly aromatic and easily extracted constituents and highest alcohol concentrations for difficult to extract constituents (bark, root, and seed tinctures often use 60% alcohol).

Tinctures made with fresh plant also require higher alcohol content (usually 60% to 95%) due to the water contained within the fresh plant. Extracting resins from cottonwood buds requires a minimum 75% alcohol, as in grain alcohol/Everclear brand.

For nutritive tonic tinctures, a dropperful is generally taken. For doses for specific herbs, consult with an herbalist to determine the dose right for you. For some herbs, the dosage is merely drops!

GLOSSARY

Alga: any of a number of chlorophyll-containing organisms that live in fresh or salt water. Algae may be one-celled or many-celled, such as those plants we commonly call "seaweed."

Alkaloid: a nitrogen-containing organic compound that is insoluble in water. Alkaloids are generally bitter and usually potentially toxic.

Analgesic: pain-relieving.

Anthocyanins: a plant flavonoid pigment (red, blue, or violet in color), associated with anti-inflammatory benefits.

Anticatarrhal: counteracting mucus in sinuses.

Antioxidants: substances that prevent or slow the damage to body cells caused by unstable molecules (free radicals).

Antispasmodic: a substance that relieves or prevents muscle spams.

Antiulcerogenic: preventing onset of ulcers.

Astringent: causing skin cells or other soft bodily tissues to contract.

Basal rosette: a circular arrangement of leaves at the base of a plant's stem.

Beta-carotene: an antioxidant plant pigment that converts to vitamin A.

Bioremediation: using plants or other microorganisms to break down environmental pollutants.

Bog: wet spongy acidic ground, containing sphagnum, sedges, and moisture-loving species.

Catkin: a male or female drooping, spike-like cluster of flowers.

Chemopreventive: agents that inhibit development of cancer.

Cirrhosis: liver disease with irreversible scarring, often caused by excess alcohol or viral hepatitis.

Composite: flowers containing both ray and disk petals.

Corm: a swollen underground plant stem that stores nutrients.

Decoction: an herbal preparation made by boiling an herb in water. Decoctions are often used with bark, roots, large seeds, and other hard plant materials.

Demulcent: a substance that soothes mucous membranes and other irritated tissues.

Dermatitis: inflammation of the skin.

Diaphoretic: having power to increase sweating.

Diuretic: promoting release of excess fluid, urine.

Edema: swelling caused by excess fluid in body tissues.

Ethnobotany: the scientific study of traditional plant knowledge.

Expectorant: an agent that encourages discharge of mucus from the lungs.

Exudate: a substance that oozes from injured plants, such as resins, gums, oils.

Flavonoids: plant phytonutrient (plant chemical) associated with health benefits ranging from blood sugar regulation to brain function.

Flower essence: a floral infusion used as a vibrational catalyst for emotional or spiritual healing.

Genera: the plural of genus.

Genus: the subdivision of a plant family, typically consisting of more than one species.

Goiter: noncancerous thyroid gland enlargement.

Hepatitis: inflammation of the liver.

Hepatoprotective: the ability to protect the liver from damage.

Holdfast: a root-like attachment that anchors algae to a rock or other surface.

Hyperthyroidism: abnormally high thyroid gland activity.

Hypothyroidism: abnormally low thyroid gland activity.

Homeopathy: a branch of medicine based on the "law of similars" in which minute quantities of substances (specially prepared through shaking and dilution) are used to eliminate symptoms that the same substances (if given on a large scale) would otherwise cause in a healthy person.

Hyperlipidaemia: high cholesterol.

Immunomodulatory: an agent that modifies immune system response.

Infusion: an herbal preparation made by pouring boiling water over an herb and steeping; often used with leaves, flowers, and small seeds.

Lactation: milk secretion from mammary glands.

Liniment: an external herbal preparation prepared by steeping herbs in a solvent such as rubbing alcohol or brandy.

Mucilage: the thick slippery substance in plants that stores water.

Osteoprotective: bone-protective.

Phytoremediation: the use of plants to remove pollutants from air, water, or soil.

Palmate: a leaf divided into leaflets radiating from a central point.

Pinnate: a compound leaf with leaflets arranged on two sides of a stem or long axis.

Phytoestrogen: a plant substance that binds to the estrogen receptors, thus stimulating estrogen production.

Pistil: the female organ of a flower, composed of the seed-bearing ovary, the style (stalk), and the stigma (which receives the pollen).

Plaster: a paste-like herbal mixture applied to the body to promote healing.

Potherb: a cooked vegetable.

Poultice: an external herbal preparation made by crushing or bruising plants and applying them (sometimes heated and/or wrapped in cloth) directly to the skin.

Proanthocyanidin: a type of flavonoid.

Prostrate: trailing along the ground.

Purgative: an agent that promotes bowel evacuation.

Quercetin: a flavonoid found in many plants.

Rhizome: modified underground stems, aka creeping rootstalks.

Sepal: the outer, usually green, part of the flower that protects the developing bud.

Shingles: a viral disease characterised by painful skin blisters, usually around the waist or face

Sporophyll: the leaf blades that produce spores.

Shrubs: woody plants smaller than trees with multiple branches.

Species: a group of plants that interbreed freely and have many characteristics in common.

Stamen: the male fertilizing floral organ, typically consisting of the pollen-producing anther and a stalk (filament).

Tincture: an herbal preparation made by steeping an herb in a menstruum (solvent) such as brandy, glycerin, or vinegar.

Tonic: a substance, such as an herb, used to strengthen body systems (often of a preventive nature).

Umbel: an umbrella-shaped flower in which all the flower stalks arise from one point.

Whorl: an arrangement of plant parts radiating from a central point.

RECOMMENDED READING & RESOURCES

For a full list of footnotes to this book, visit www.westmarginpress.com/book-details/9781513262789/alaskas-wild-plants-revised-edition/

ALASKA

Fienup-Riordan, Ann, Alice Rearden, Marie Meade, and Kevin Jernigan. *Nunam Qaingani Nautulit Nertukngait Iinruktukngait-llu Edible and Medicinal Plants of Southwest Alaska*. Calista Education and Culture, Inc. April 2019.

Fortuine, Robert, M.D., M.P.H. *Alaska Medicine*. "The Use of Medicinal Plants by the Alaska Natives." Vol. 30, No. 6, November/December 1988.

Garza, Dolly. *Common Edible Seaweeds in the Gulf of Alaska*. Fairbanks: Alaska Sea Grant

Garibaldi, Ann. *Medicinal Flora of the Alaska Natives: A Compilation of Knowledge from Literary Sources of Aleut, Alutiiq, Athabascan, Eyak, Haida, Inupiat, Tlingit, Tsimshian, and Yupik Traditional Healing Methods Using Plants*. Anchorage: University of Alaska Anchorage, Alaska Natural Heritage Program, 1999.

Hultén, Eric. *Flora of Alaska and Neighboring Territories*. Stanford: Stanford University Press, 1968.

Jones, Anore. *Plants That We Eat. Nauriat Nigiñaqtuat, From the traditional Wisdom of the Iñupiat Elders of Northwest Alaska*. Fairbanks Alaska: University of Alaska Press, 2010.

Kari, Priscilla Russell. *Tanaina Plantlore, Dena'ina K'et'una*. Alaska Region: National Park Service, 1987.

Kelso, Fran. *Plant Lore of an Alaskan Island: Foraging in the Kodiak Archepelago*, AuthorHouse, 2011

Laursen, Gary A. and Neil McArthur. *Alaska's Mushrooms: A Wide-Ranging Guide*. Portland: Graphic Arts Books, 2016.

Pratt, Verna E. *Field Guide to Alaskan Wildflowers*. Anchorage: Alaskakrafts Publishing, 1989.

Schofield, Janice J. *Discovering Wild Plants*. Anchorage: Eaton/Todd Communications, 2014.

Viereck, Eleanor G. *Alaska's Wilderness Medicines*. Portland: Alaska Northwest Books, 1991.

EDIBLE & MEDICINAL PLANTS

Brown, Tom, Jr. *Tom Brown's Guide to Wild Edible and Medicinal Plants*. New York: Berkley Books, 1985.

Buhner, Stephen Harrod. *Sacred and Herbal Healing Beers*. Boulder, Colorado: Siris Books, 1998.

Elpel, Thomas J. *Botany in a Day: The Patterns Method of Plant Identification*. Pony, MT: Hops Press, 2013.

Gladstar, Rosemary. *Rosemary Gladstar's Medicinal Herbs*. N. Adams Mass: Storey Press, 2012.

Goldfrank, L.R. (ed). *Goldfrank's Toxicologic Emergencies*. 7th Edition. New York: McGraw-Hill, 2002.

Gray, Beverly. *The Boreal Herbal*. Yukon: Aurora Borealis Press, 2011.

Harrington, H.D. *Western Edible Wild Plants*. The University of New Mexico Press, 1972.

Hellson, John C. *Ethnobotany of the Blackfoot Indians*. Ottawa, Ontario: National Museums of Canada, 1974.

Kletter, Christa and Monika Kriechbaum (ed). *Tibetan Medicinal Plants*. Germany: Medpharm, 2001.

Li, Shih-Chen. *Chinese Medicinal Herbs: A Modern Edition of a Classic Sixteenth-Century Manual*. Mineola, New York: Dover Publications, 1973.

Moerman. D. *Native American Ethnobotany*. Oregon: Timber Press, 1998.

Turner, N.J., L.C. Thompson, and M.T. Thompson *Thompson Ethnobotany: Knowledge and Usage of Plants by the Thompson Indians of British Columbia*. Victoria, British Columbia: Royal British Columbia Museum, 1990.

Small, Ernest. *North American Cornucopia: Top 100 Indigenous Food Plants*. New York: CRC Press: 2014.

NATIVE, INTRODUCED & INVASIVE SPECIES

Benfield, William. *At War with Nature*. Amazon, 2015.

Buhner, Stephen Harrod. *Healing Lyme*. New Mexico: Raven Press, 2016.

Orion, Tao. *Beyond the War on Invasive Species*. White River Junction, VT: Chelsea Green Publishing, 2015.

Pearce, Fred. *The New Wild*. Duxford, UK: Icon Books, 2016.

Scott, Timothy Lee. *Invasive Plant Medicine*. Rochester, VT: Healing Arts Press, 2010.

WEBSITES (mentioned in citations)

Plant Identification, Edible Plants, Weed Ecology, Mushrooms, and more: www.wildflowers-and-weeds.com

American Botanical Council, "Your source for reliable herbal medicine information": www.herbalgram.com

Ryan Drum aka "Fucus man" articles: www.ryandrum.com/articles.htm

Seaweeds of Alaska: www.seaweedsofalaska.com

Herbs A-Z (some Alaskan species) by Medical Herbalist Richard Whelan: www.rjwhelan.co.nz

Finnish herbalist Henriette Kress' "bark side" herbal information site: www.henriettes-herb.com

Alaskan flower and environmental essences: alaskanessences.com

Online classes for plant identification: www.botanyeveryday.com/online-classes

Green Deane's photo-illustrated cattail preparation and much more: www.eattheweeds.com/cattails-a-survival-dinner/

Plant Names in Indigenous Languages by University of Victoria: https://dspace.library.uvic.ca/bitstream/handle/1828/5091/Appendix%20 2B%20%20UVicSpace%20Indigenous%20names%20of%20native%20 species_BIG.pdf?sequence=5&isAllowed=y

BLOGS (An assortment of wild foods blogs referenced.)

Wild food, wild medicine, wild living, and the old ways of doing and being: monicawilde.com

"Food and medicine from nature": www.alaskafloatsmyboat.com/food-and-medicine-from-nature

"Foraging resources, including specifics on fermented fireweed tea": honest-food.net/foraging-recipes/

"Welcome to wild food heaven": www.gallowaywildfoods.com

"The forager's feast": www.ledameredith.com

Photo-illustrated birch syrup process: joybileefarm.com/birch-syrup/

"Adventures of a 21st century forager": fat-of-the-land.blogspot.com

Alan Bergo's recipe for yarrow and much more: foragerchef.com/cooking-with-yarrow/

ONLINE VIDEOS (Illustrating processes mentioned in *Alaska's Wild Plants*)

The process of roasting cleavers for coffee: youtu.be/cLYWhMDhwDs

Making birch syrup: alaskabirchsyrup.com/birch-syrup-videos/

Making birch bark flour: video-shield.mediavine.com/video/upload/ sp_mediavine_hd_h264/v1554830606/looche3scdtytf1ywins.m3u8

Make juniper beverage: balkanlunchbox.com/fermented-juniper-berry-juice-smreka/

Make juniper beverage: thetartart.wordpress.com/2016/02/27/smreka/

Cleaning fiddlehead ferns: youtu.be/O1O67-TUogE

HERBAL DIRECTORY

ALASKA CLASSES

Alaska Native Tribal Health Consortium
anthc.org/what-we-do/traditional-foods-and-nutrition/alaskan-plants-as-food-medicine/
ANTHC hosts regional symposiums promoting traditional plant knowledge and ethical harvesting, as well as the Store Outside Your Door project with numerous videos.

Anam Cara
www.nancylee-evans.com/wild-herbalism
This resource is for those interested in wildcrafting Alaska plants as food and medicine, and developing spiritual connections with the plants.

Good Earth Garden School
www.goodearthgardenschool.com
Ellen Vande Visse is the guru of compost and organic soil fertility and also teaches classes in communicating with plants. She utilizes the Findhorn-Perelandra-style of co-creation with nature. Read more in her book, *Ask Mother Nature, a Conscious Gardener's Guide.*

Gayla Pedersen
For Kodiak Island plant lore enthusiasts, check for classes depending on the season and availability by emailing Gayla at Gayla.pedersen@gmail.com.

ALASKAN HERBAL ASSOCIATIONS & PUBLICATIONS

Kenai Peninsula Mycological Society
www.facebook.com/KenaiPennisulaMushroomSociety/
Learn about the study of mushrooms and lichens.

Alaska Native Plant Society
www.aknps.org
The Alaska Native Plant Society hosts native plant walks and features abundant resources.

ALASKAN HERBAL PRODUCTS & FLOWER ESSENCES

Maiden Alaska Herbals
www.maidenalaskaherbals.com
Learn about ethically harvested, high-quality Alaskan herbal products.

Alaskan Essences
www.alaskanessences.com
Find high-quality flower and environmental essences from Alaska.

Village Herbals
www.villageherbalsalaska.com
Learn about quality handmade Alaskan herbal products for the whole family.

SEEDS

Directory of Alaska Native Plant Sources
http://plants.alaska.gov/nativeplantindex.htm
Visit for an extensive list of sources for Alaskan wildflowers, herbs, trees, etc.

HERBAL CLASSES, SCHOOLS & APPRENTICE PROGRAMS OUTSIDE ALASKA

California School of Herbal Studies
9309 California 116, Forestville, CA 95436
www.cshs.com
This is one of the oldest herbal education centers in North America, founded 1978 by Rosemary Gladstar.

The Science and Art of Herbalism
https://scienceandartofherbalism.com
Find an online study course with Rosemary Gladstar.

Foundations in Herbal Medicine with Dr. Tieraona Lowdog
https://www.medicinelodgeranch.com/products/foundations-in-herbal-medicine
Over 500 hours of multimedia resources on herbal medicine are available.

INDEX

ACKNOWLEDGMENTS

ACKNOWLEDGMENTS

Every book has a behind-the-scenes support team, and this edition is no exception. Gratitude to my patient, good-natured husband Barry Eaton, who covered countless tasks while I exited into the world of book revision and deadlines. Huge thanks to the fantastic team at West Margin Press, editor Olivia Ngai, "guru" designer Rachel Metzger, and enthusiastic publicist Angie Zbornik, as well as publishing director Jennifer Newens, indexer Sam Arnold-Boyd, and editor Susan Sommer, for their support in bringing this edition to life. Herbalist Gayla Pederson of Kodiak shared support as enthusiastic "first reader" of the revised edition. Deepest thanks to Louise Desclos for her sharp photographic eye and edits, and to John Desclos, Vivian Desclos Glass, and Rodney Glass for technical help and generous support. Kudos to Robyn Klein of Bozeman, Montana, for perceptive herbal edits, and to Thomas Elpel of Pony, Montana, for answering taxonomy queries. Thanks to Ann Fienup-Riordan for sharing Yup'ik plant knowledge, including information on regional mare's tail use. Appreciation to Kim Aspelund for sharing herbal knowledge and Eyak Indian resources. Appreciation to Barbara Cellarius, Doug Deut, and Tom Thornton for tracking down information on fern root use by Yakutat Tlingit. Thanks to all my herbal teachers and mentors, including Rosemary Gladstar and Dr. Tierarona-Lowdog. Enduring gratitude to the plants themselves for sharing so generously throughout the generations, and to all my herbal students whose insights have contributed to this work. Thanks too to countless unnamed in my international support team, who I love dearly.

I am also grateful to Stephanie McKee, and Ellen Vandevisse for edits on "Reflections on Native, Introduced and Invasive Species" and to Joe Roman, PhD, for permission to include his line: "Eat the Invaders One Bite at a Time." Due to space limitations of this pocket guide, "Reflections" as well as "Connecting with Plants" and "Introducing Children to Wild Plants" was not included but is available on blog: "At Home with Janice Schofield Eaton." And a free download of all resources cited in the revision of *Alaska's Wild Plants* is available from West Margin Press.